GRABOVOI

The Healing Matrix

+ 700 Cheat codes to the universe

The Grabovoi Code:
Numbers That Heal, Prosper
and Transform

Exclusive : + 700 Codes in 4 languages
English, French , Spanish and Russian
From page 24 to 109
(код на русском языке со страницы 24 по 109)

Pre-Released on 14th November 2023 , day of Birthday of G. Grabovoï

Sommaire (in French, only chapter 5, en français + de 700 codes Grabovoi):

Introduction: The Life of Grigori Grabovoi

1. Early Life and Education page 7

- Birth and childhood background.
- Academic pursuits and early interests.
- Initial encounters with the concepts of healing and numerology.

2. Development of the Grabovoi Number System page 9

- The inception of Grabovoi's unique numerical system.
- How personal experiences and research led to the development of this system.
- The process of assigning specific numbers to various life aspects.

3. Philosophies and Influences page 11

- Overview of the philosophical underpinnings of Grabovoi's work.
- Influences from traditional and contemporary thought leaders.
- Integration of spiritual, scientific, and metaphysical concepts.

4. Controversies and Criticisms

- Discussion of the skepticism and controversies surrounding Grabovoi's methods.
- Responses to criticisms from both scientific and spiritual communities.
- Analysis of the legal and ethical implications of his teachings.

Chapters Outline with codes in 4 languages

Chapter 6: Advanced Techniques and Combinations -   page 109

- Complex sequences for specific and advanced goals.
- Integrating numbers into daily routines and practices.
- Case studies and expert insights with **hormones.**
- **Adrenaline, Dopamine, Oxytocin, Serotonin**   page 111

Chapter 7: The Future of Grabovoi Numbers   -   page 112

- Potential developments and evolving practices.
- Integration into modern holistic and alternative therapies
- Vaccine Protection code ! **page 114**

How to use Grabovoi numbers (summary)   page 115

Other Spiritual Enlightenment Books   **page 117**

1. Early Life and Education : *Grigori Petrovich Grabovoi*

In the understated, often overlooked village of **Bogara** in **Kazakhstan,** a land more renowned for its expansive steppes than for birthing luminaries, **Grigori Petrovich Grabovoi** came into the world on the *14th of November, 1963*. In a place where life was as vast as the landscape, this **Russian mathematician**'s entrance was not marked by cosmic spectacles or heavenly fanfare. Yet, in the realm of numerology, it was an event of profound significance. Unbeknownst to many, a future maestro of numbers had just drawn his first breath. **Grigori,** now a *60-year-old man*, stands as a towering figure in the eyes of many. To some, he is a genius, a seer, a healer, a *"true master"* - an individual whose presence in the world of numbers and beyond is nothing short of immense.

Grigori's childhood was as ordinary as it gets, if you discount the fact that he could probably count the stars in the sky faster than his peers could count their marbles. His early years were speckled with the usual joys and perils of childhood, from skinned knees to the mysteries of the abacus. And while other children were content playing hide-and-seek, young **Grigori** was more inclined to seek the hidden patterns of the universe.

As he sauntered, rather unassumingly, through the hallways of academia, **Grigori**'s appetite for knowledge grew. His mind, a sponge in a sea of numbers, soaked up mathematical theories and scientific postulations with an ease that left his teachers both astounded and slightly unnerved. While his classmates wrestled with the intricacies of algebra, **Grigori** was waltzing through complex equations as if they were nursery rhymes.

It was during these formative years that **Grigori**'s fascination with the healing arts began to intertwine with his numerical prowess. Picture a young lad, head buried in books by day, gazing at the stars by night, and you have a rather picturesque, if not entirely accurate, image of our protagonist. The concepts of healing and numerology began to dance a curious tango in his mind, each step leading him closer to his future revelations.

Initial encounters with healing were less about bandages and balms and more about the balm of the universe - numbers. **Grigori**, with the earnestness of a scholar and the curiosity of a cat, began to toy with <u>the idea that numbers held more power than just to add and subtract.</u> **<u>They could heal, transform, and perhaps even transcend the physical realm.</u>**

In these youthful explorations, **Grigori** was like a young alchemist, his laboratory the world, his ingredients numbers and their infinite combinations. Each discovery was a stepping stone, each question a portal to new realms of possibility.

And so, dear reader, our stage is set. From these humble beginnings, a maestro of numerical healing was emerging, ready to challenge the very fabric of reality with nothing but a chalkboard and his extraordinary vision.

This playful and imaginative introduction to **Grabovoi**'s early life sets the tone for a book that is not just informative but also a delight to read, inviting readers to explore the fascinating journey of Grigori **Grabovoi** with a sense of wonder and curiosity.

There is a code for Everything, **8 910 194 918 808**. Against phobia… painless childbirth: **5 421 555,** vitamin deficiency: **5 451 234,** even a number to reduce crime in Cities **978 14 32 18** or avoid traffic accidents **111 79.**

If you desire more codes, go to *Chapter 5* (page 25); everything is available in four languages. Welcome to the numbers that heal. This book is now also available with code translations in *English, German, Chinese, Japanese, and Arabic traditions and specific French, Spanish, Italian and even Swedish 100% edition.*

2. Development of the Grabovoi Number System

In the halls of mathematical lore, where numbers dance and formulas play, **Grigori Grabovoi,** a modern-day numerical alchemist, began to stir a pot that would bubble with the most peculiar of concoctions. He wasn't just adding one and one to make two; oh no, he was on a quest to make one and one make a universe.

The inception of **Grabovoi**'s unique numerical system didn't happen in a thunderous moment of epiphany, nor was it delivered on stone tablets from a mountaintop. Instead, it unfolded like a delicate origami, each fold a revelation, each crease a new understanding of how numbers could transcend their arithmetic shackles.

Grigori's personal journey was as essential to this development as ink is to a pen. He delved into the mysteries of numerology with the fervor of a detective in a whodunit novel. His research was not confined to dusty tomes or echoey libraries; it sprawled across the canvas of life. He observed, he questioned, he pondered. From the symphony of the stars to the rhythm of a heartbeat, he sought the numerical threads that wove the tapestry of existence.

The process of assigning specific numbers to various life aspects was not unlike a composer assigning notes to a symphony. Each number was a note, and together, they composed a melody that resonated with the energies of health, wealth, love, and more. **Grigori**'s system wasn't just about numbers; it was about harmony, about the cosmic music that plays silently in the background of our lives.

Imagine, if you will, a world where numbers are not just symbols on a page but keys that unlock the mysteries of the universe. In **Grabovoi**'s hands, numbers became more than just tools for counting; they transformed into a language that spoke directly to the fabric of reality. He saw in numbers a potential to heal, to change, to empower. To him, numbers were alive, pulsating with energy and possibility.

As he assigned numbers to aspects of life, **Grigori** was like a gardener planting seeds in a cosmic garden. Each number was a seed, and when nurtured with belief and understanding, it would bloom into a flower of desired manifestation. He mapped the numbers to ailments, emotions, desires, creating a lexicon that bridged the gap between the tangible and intangible, the physical and metaphysical.

His work was a tapestry where science and spirituality intertwined, a fusion that often raised eyebrows in both camps. Skeptics scoffed, enthusiasts marveled, but **Grabovoi,** undeterred, continued to weave his numerical magic, driven by a vision that transcended mere calculation.

To the untrained eye, his methods might have seemed like plucking numbers from a cosmic lottery. But to those who looked closer, there was method in this numerical madness. It was a dance of intuition, insight, and intellect, a dance where numbers twirled and leaped in the grand ballroom of existence.

And so, our intrepid numerologist marched on, charting a course through uncharted waters, with numbers as his compass and an unwavering belief in their power as his guiding star. In the universe according to **Grabovoi,** numbers were not just quantities; they were qualities, each carrying a unique vibration, a unique song.

In this brave new world, the number seven wasn't just a number; it was a whisper of infinity, a hint of the divine. The number three was not merely a trio; it was a symbol of harmony, balance, and growth. And as for one, well, it was the beginning, the very essence of being, the first note in the symphony of existence.

This imaginative and engaging narrative style brings to life the intriguing process behind the development of **Grabovoi's** number system, inviting readers to not just understand but to feel the wonder and potential that Grigori **Grabovoi** saw in the world of numbers.

3. Philosophies and Influences

In the grand tapestry of **Grabovoi**'s world, where numbers were not mere digits but the **DNA of the universe**, his philosophies shimmered like threads of gold. They were not born in the vacuum of a solitary mind; rather, they were a mosaic, pieced together with fragments of wisdom from sages past and present.

Grigori Grabovoi, our numerical virtuoso, didn't just pluck his ideas from the ether. Oh no, he was a collector of thoughts, a curator of philosophies. His mind was a grand library, echoing with the voices of ancient mystics and modern scientists alike. **Plato** might have talked about the world of forms, but **Grabovoi**'s world was one of numbers – a universe where every form had a number, and every number, a hidden power.

From the mystic twirls of Sufi dervishes to the stern equations of Einstein, **Grabovoi**'s influences were as varied as the colors in a prism. He wove the teachings of **Pythagoras**, who saw numbers in everything, with the insights of **Carl Jung**, who saw everything in symbols. To this eclectic mix, he added a dash of quantum physics and a sprinkle of Eastern spirituality, creating a philosophical cocktail that was both heady and invigorating.

His work was a bridge between the old and the new, the seen and the unseen. Where traditional thought ended, and contemporary ideas began, **Grabovoi** built his castle. This castle wasn't made of stones and mortar; it was built from the intangible bricks of belief, intuition, and imagination.

In the grand bazaar of ideas, **Grabovoi** was a discerning shopper. He perused the stalls of spiritual teachings, selecting the finest spices of wisdom. He visited the workshops of scientific minds, handpicking the tools of logic and reason. From these varied expeditions, he returned with a trove of treasures, which he melded into his unique philosophical framework.

This framework wasn't just a dry collection of theories and postulates. It was alive, pulsating with the energy of a thousand thoughts. In it, science and spirituality danced a tango of cosmic proportions. They were no longer adversaries, vying for the throne of truth. In **Grabovoi**'s universe, they were partners, twirling gracefully around the dance floor of understanding.

Grabovoi's integration of spiritual, scientific, and metaphysical concepts was like a chef creating a new recipe. He took the spiritual essence of faith, the scientific rigor of inquiry, and the metaphysical wonder of the unknown, and mixed them together. The result was a dish that was as nourishing to the soul as it was appetizing to the intellect.

In this philosophical feast, each concept had its place. The spiritual teachings lent depth and soul, reminding us that numbers were more than quantities; they were keys to unlocking the deeper mysteries of existence. The scientific principles added structure and credibility, ensuring that the flight of fancy was always grounded in the realm of possibility. And the metaphysical elements? They added the spice, the magic, the hint of something beyond, something just out of the reach of our understanding.

And so, dear reader, we find ourselves in the midst of a philosophical odyssey, guided by a man who saw the world not as it was, but as it could be – a world where numbers were not just the language of the universe, but the melody of a song waiting to be sung. This section, paints a vivid picture of the diverse philosophical and intellectual influences that shaped **Grabovoi**'s unique approach, inviting readers to explore the intricate and fascinating world he envisioned.

Chapter 1: Fundamentals of Grabovoi Numbers

In a world where numbers are often relegated to the mundane tasks of counting and calculating, the **Grabovoi** number system emerges like a phoenix from the ashes of arithmetic, offering a glimpse into a realm where numbers are not just figures, but whispers of a deeper cosmic language.

The ABCs of Grabovoi's Numerology

Let's start at the beginning, shall we? In the alphabet of **Grabovoi**'s universe, numbers are the letters. But these aren't your run-of-the-mill digits that sit idly on a page. Oh no. In **Grabovoi**'s hands, numbers are akin to magical incantations, each one holding the power to heal, transform, and even, dare we say, perform the miraculous.

But how, you ask, do these mystical numbers work? Picture this: each number, from the humble '1' to the lofty '9', is imbued with specific energies and vibrations. They are like tiny engines of the universe, humming with potential and power. When strung together in a sequence, these numbers create a symphony of vibrations that resonate with the energies of the universe, tapping into its vast reservoir of healing and transformation.

Interpreting the Cosmic Code

Now, wielding these numbers is not like waving a magic wand and expecting rabbits to pop out of hats. It requires understanding, intention, and a dash of faith. To interpret these numbers is to engage in a conversation with the universe, where each digit is a word, each sequence a sentence, laden with meaning and purpose.

Incorporating **Grabovoi** numbers into daily life is akin to learning a new language, a language where numbers are not just symbols, but keys to unlocking the doors of reality. **Want to heal a headache?** There's a number for that: **481 85 43 Seeking love?** There's a sequence for that too: **888 412 128 90 18** . Each number, each combination, serves a purpose, like signposts on the road to well-being and fulfillment. Tales of Transformation: Testimonials and Anecdotes

Of course, such claims of numerical wizardry are bound to raise eyebrows and elicit sceptical frowns. But hark! The tales of those who've walked the **Grabovoi** path speak volumes. These aren't just cold, hard facts and figures; these are stories of real people, real experiences – anecdotes that twinkle with the light of truth and possibility.

There's the tale of the businessman, down on his luck, who used **Grabovoi** numbers to turn his fortunes around. Like a phoenix rising from the ashes of bankruptcy, his enterprise soared, all thanks to a carefully chosen sequence of digits. Or consider the story of the young woman, plagued by heartaches, who found love in the most unexpected of places, guided by the gentle nudge of a **Grabovoi** number sequence. Her tale is not just one of romance but of faith and **serendipity**, woven together by the invisible threads of numerical destiny.

And let's not forget the countless stories of health restored, dreams achieved, and lives transformed, all through the simple, yet profound act of aligning with the **vibrational** symphony of **Grabovoi** numbers.

In this whirlwind tour of the fundamentals of **Grabovoi**'s system, we've merely scratched the surface of a world **where numbers are the conduit to a life of greater health,** abundance, and joy. As we close this chapter, remember, dear reader, in the universe of **Grabovoi** numbers, the mundane becomes magical, the impossible becomes possible, and the numbers, oh, the numbers, they dance with the very essence of life itself. **<u>Writing specific number 716</u>** on a water bottle is very powerful, it's water memory.

Chapter 2: Healing with Numbers

In the grand tapestry of life, where each thread represents a moment, a feeling, a breath, the **Grabovoi** numbers weave their magic, offering healing and hope. This isn't just a tale of numbers; it's a story of restoration, rejuvenation, and perhaps a touch of the miraculous.

A Numeric Pharmacy for Physical Ailments

Imagine, if you will, a pharmacy where the shelves are lined not with bottles and pills but with sequences of numbers, each a potion for a different ailment. This is the **Grabovoi** approach to physical healing. Have a headache? There's a number for that. Suffering from a bout of the flu? Yes, there's a number for that too. From the common cold to the more grievous of maladies, the **Grabovoi** system offers a numerical remedy, a vibrational balm to soothe and heal.

These numbers, however, aren't just plucked from thin air. They are carefully crafted, each digit a specific vibration that resonates with the body's own healing frequencies. It's like tuning a piano, but instead of keys and strings, we're working with cells and energies.

Mending the Mind: Emotional and Psychological Healing

But what of the wounds that are unseen, the scars that lie not on the body but on the heart and mind? Fear not, for **Grabovoi** numbers venture into these realms too. Numbers for heartache, for anxiety, for those days when the weight of the world feels a tad too heavy on your shoulders.

Using these numbers for emotional and psychological healing is like having a conversation with your soul, where each sequence is a word of comfort, a gesture of understanding. It's not about denying the complexities of human emotions but about offering a tool, a beacon of light in the darker corridors of the mind.

The Art of Prevention: Numbers for Overall Wellness

And then there's the art of prevention, for why wait for the storm when one can dance in the calm? The **Grabovoi** numbers offer a preventive approach to wellness, a way to keep the body and mind in harmonious balance. These sequences are like the daily vitamins of the soul, nourishing and fortifying against the trials and tribulations of life.

Whether it's a number to boost immunity, one to enhance vitality, or a sequence to maintain mental clarity, the idea is to use these numbers not just as a cure but as a shield, a protective embrace in the dance of life.

In this chapter, we've journeyed through the healing potential of **Grabovoi** numbers (*see from page 23 for more*) , exploring their use in addressing physical ailments, emotional turmoils, and the pursuit of overall wellness. It's a narrative where numbers are not mere digits but vessels of healing, each carrying the promise of better health, peace of mind, and a life lived in vibrant harmony.

In this chapter, we have woven a narrative tapestry that brings to life the healing potential of **Grabovoi** numbers, portraying them as tools for physical, emotional, and preventive care, all told with a touch of whimsy and wonder.

Chapter 3: Manifesting Abundance and Success : 318 798

In the enchanting universe of **Grabovoi** numbers, where digits dance and destiny is written in numerical codes, we find ourselves at the crossroads of material wealth and spiritual enlightenment. This isn't just a tale of rags to riches; it's a journey of transformation, a ballet of balance between the tangible and the ethereal.

The Numerical Keys to Financial Prosperity

Picture a world where your bank account is as healthy as your body and mind, where prosperity flows as freely as a river, nourished by the rains of **Grabovoi** numbers. These numbers aren't just random sequences; they are the alchemical formulas for financial success. Looking for a raise at work? There's a number for that. Dreaming of a successful business venture? Oh, you bet there's a number for that.

But it's not about chanting numbers and waiting for a windfall. It's about aligning your energy with the vibrations of abundance, about tuning your personal frequency to the symphony of prosperity. In **Grabovoi**'s world, numbers are the conductors of this symphony, guiding the orchestra of the universe to play the melody of your financial dreams.

Harmonizing Material Wealth with Spiritual Growth

Now, let's not forget the soul in our pursuit of gold. For what is wealth without wisdom, riches without reflection? **Grabovoi** numbers offer more than just material gains; they are a bridge between financial success and spiritual growth.

It's a delicate dance, balancing the pursuit of wealth with the nourishment of the spirit. But fear not, for these numbers are like skilled tightrope walkers, effortlessly striding the line between the two. They teach us that true abundance comes not just from a full wallet but from a fulfilled soul.

Tales of Transformation: From Numbers to Nirvana

And now, dear reader, let's bask in the tales of those who've walked this path of numerical abundance. Stories of individuals who, armed with a sequence of digits, turned their fortunes around, not just in bank statements but in life itself.

There's the tale of the struggling artist, who, with a **Grabovoi** number clutched in hand, found her paintings sought after by galleries far and wide. Her story is not just one of financial gain but of artistic recognition and self-fulfillment.

Or consider the young entrepreneur, weighed down by debts and doubts, who discovered in **Grabovoi** numbers the key to unlock his potential. His business didn't just survive; it thrived, blossoming into an empire of innovation and impact.

In these stories of transformation and success, we see not just the power of numbers but the strength of belief, the courage of conviction. They remind us that in the grand bazaar of life, **Grabovoi** numbers are the coins with which we purchase our dreams.

In this chapter, we've journeyed through the mystical landscape of **Grabovoi** numbers, exploring their role in manifesting financial prosperity and career success, while balancing material wealth with spiritual growth. Through engaging storytelling, we've highlighted the transformative power of these numbers, painting a picture of a world where abundance is not just a possibility, but a vibrational reality.

Chapter 4: Personal Relationships and Harmony: how to do it?

In the mystical universe of **Grabovoi** numbers, where each digit sings a song of connection and understanding, we find a treasure trove of sequences dedicated to the art of relationships. Here, we present the keys to unlocking harmony, love, and understanding in the intricate dance of human connections.

To use it, first, you have to activate it then visualize, recite or write numbers to get its energy for manifestation. **Grabovoi** Codes are a powerful tool for manifesting anything desired in life!

Let's begin with the most important aspect of these practices nowadays:

- *__Say these numbers as affirmations, with a good heart, and with gratitude.__*

- Listen to your **Grabovoi** sequence and repeat the numbers 28 times. For example 461 05 67 for winning the lottery.

- Focus on the numbers by looking at them **for 5 minutes.**

- Memorize the sequence and repeat them multiple times throughout the day.

- Write it on a piece of paper **28 times.**

To use these codes, it is important to first focus on what you desire and then recite the corresponding code out loud with a clear intention. It is important to note that the power codes should be recited __out loud with focus and conviction__ in order to experience powerful and lasting results.

1./ WORLD TOOL BOX

Peace	**100 110 50 10**
Solution asap	741
Stop catastrophe	**178 41 21**
Clear weather	888 71 843 21
Avoid Accidents	111 79
Addiction	53 333 53
Change your reality	608 841 228

2./ LOVE & ROMANCE

Finding True Love:	**528 491**
Self Esteem	481 89 17 49 814
Self Love	**39 68 15**
Bring couch to me:	899 744 76
Deepening Romantic Relationships:	**639 217**
Reigniting Passion:	987 654
Love for a Boyfriend:	**23 789 283**
Manifest Love (fast)	888 412 128 9018
Eternal Love	**888 912 818 848**
Romance & Sex	401 543 512

Get your ex back	**899 744 76**
Specific Person	986 115
Bring my love back to me	**385 67 94**
To attract a partner	197 023
For self-love	**396 815**
For self Esteem	481 895 17 49 814
Manifesting Romance	**401 543 5 12**
Manifesting your ideal future	813 791
Dream Body	**824 06 92**
Charisma and sexual magnetism	49 17 18 59 48 17
Increase libido	**598 6179 184 91**
Marriage	48 04 03 05
Attract Specific Person	**986 11 5**
Twin Flame / Soul Mate	924 01 78
Rekindle the Spark in a Relationship	**874 912**
To heal a broken heart	74 89 77 86
Forgiveness	**124 69 908**
Unconditional Love	478 90 12

3./ Numbers for FAMILY & HARMONY

Strengthening Family Bonds: **562 3 1892**

Resolving Family Conflicts: **843 31457**

Nurturing Parent-Child Relationships: **518 49 13 19**

Numbers for FRIENDSHIPS
Attracting Positive Friendships: **11 6 5 4 123**

Healing Broken Friendships: **591 8142 1814**

Deepening Mutual Understanding: **814 215 84**

Communication: **01 28 577 20**

Numbers for Overcoming Relationship Challenges

Overcoming Misunderstandings: **861 75 649**

Healing After a Breakup: **432 15 67**

Rebuilding Trust: **951 84 321**

To strengthen the Bond with your partner: **147 89 01 8**

Numbers for Fostering Deeper Connections

Enhancing Empathy and Compassion: **812 345 7**

Promoting Open and Honest Communication: **658 719 14**

Cultivating Unconditional Love: **741 852 963**

Each of these **Grabovoi** numbers carries the vibrational energy tailored to specific aspects of relationships. Whether it's the romantic whispers of love, the gentle bonds of family, the joyful camaraderie of friendships, the healing touch in times of challenge, or the deepening of connections, these numbers serve as guides and aids in the journey of relational harmony.

Remember, in the world of **Grabovoi** numbers, each sequence is a melody, playing the symphony of human connections, echoing with the tunes of love, understanding, and harmony.

For maximum results, it is recommended to start by reciting codes every day for at least 20 minutes. Techniques for implementing **Grabovoi** Codes involve **focusing on what you desire (= outcome)** and reciting the code out loud with conviction. It is important to recite the code slowly and with feeling, as this will allow the energy of the universe to work in your favor.

Advice & briefing for chapter 5, in 4 languages :

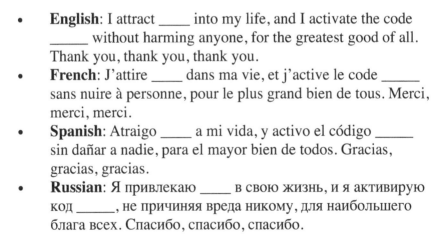

- **English**: I attract _____ into my life, and I activate the code _____ without harming anyone, for the greatest good of all. Thank you, thank you, thank you.
- **French**: J'attire _____ dans ma vie, et j'active le code _____ sans nuire à personne, pour le plus grand bien de tous. Merci, merci, merci.
- **Spanish**: Atraigo _____ a mi vida, y activo el código _____ sin dañar a nadie, para el mayor bien de todos. Gracias, gracias, gracias.
- **Russian**: Я привлекаю _____ в свою жизнь, и я активирую код _____, не причиняя вреда никому, для наибольшего блага всех. Спасибо, спасибо, спасибо.

Chapter 5 : Grabovoi Numbers : Good Health & Beyond

To begin, it is important to first focus on what you desire in life and create a clear intention. Once you have established your intention, then you can start using these codes :

Fame   827 7237
renommée, fama, слава

Good Health   808 45 700
bonne santé, buena salud, хорошее здоровье

Perfect Health   181 43 21
santé parfaite, salud perfecta, идеальное здоровье

Beauty & Physical Attraction   835 85 179

beauté et attraction physique; belleza y atracción física

Canceling negativity   474 813 2148
annuler la négativité, cancelar la negatividad
отмена негативности

Manifesting Your Ideal future   813 791
manifester votre avenir idéal, manifestar tu futuro ideal
проявление вашего идеального будущего

Self-Healing of the Body   918 79 481 81
guérison du corps; curación del cuerpo, исцеление тела

Peace   100 11 05 010
paix, Paz, мир

Chapter 5: Societal and Global Healing, extensive list

In the grand orchestra of the world, where each nation, community, and individual plays a part, the **Grabovoi numbers** emerge as the harmonizing melody, weaving together the strands of peace, understanding, and environmental stewardship.

Numbers for Community and Global Issues

Fostering Community Unity: **548 491 698 719**
Alleviating Poverty: **318 514 517 618**
Addressing Global Health Crises: **898 719 489 14**

Numbers for Promoting Peace and Understanding

Cultivating World Peace: **100 110 50 10**
Enhancing Global Cooperation: **915 481 942**
Overcoming Prejudice and Inequality: **741 32 1975**

Numbers for Environmental Healing

Restoring Environmental Balance: **973 185 412 18**
Protecting Endangered Species: **519 4812**
Combating Climate Change: **817 219 738**

Vision for a Harmonious and Balanced World

Manifesting Global Harmony: **971 83 1491**
Encouraging Sustainable Living: **812 34 57**
Building a Future of Hope and Prosperity: **318 798**

Vision to find a Dream Job

Vision pour trouver un emploi de rêve
Visión para encontrar un trabajo soñado
Видение для поиска работы мечты

Dream Job   49 3151 864 1491
Emploi de rêve
Trabajo soñado
Работа мечты

Job Offer Quickly   218 49 451 7601

Offre d'emploi rapide
Oferta de trabajo rápidamente
Быстрое предложение работы

Career Development   21 461 8319 917
Développement de carrière
Desarrollo de carrera
Развитие карьеры

Advice : *When working with **Grabovoi** Codes, it is important to use **affirmations** in conjunction with visualizations and recitation of the codes. This will help to focus your intention and increase the power of the codes. First, it is important to have a clear intention of what you wish to manifest before reciting the code. Additionally, it is beneficial **to practice visualization** when working with the codes in order to focus your intention and create the desired outcome in your mind.*

VISION for an Happy Life
VISION pour une vie heureuse
VISIÓN para una vida feliz
ВИЗИЯ счастливой жизни

Exam Success   452 16 39 83
Succès aux examens
Éxito en exámenes
Успех на экзаменах

Moving House   657 46 53
Déménagement
Mudanza
Переезд

New Car   441 44 7695
Nouvelle voiture
Coche nuevo
Новый автомобиль

Energy   245 49 20
Énergie
Energía
Энергия

Lottery Win   243 16 761
Gain à la loterie
Ganar la lotería
Выигрыш в лотерее

New Friends   722 80 400
Nouveaux amis
Nuevos amigos
Новые друзья

Increase Height
Augmenter la taille
Aumentar la altura
Увеличить рост

970 34 28

Tranquility, Balance
Tranquillité
Tranquilidad
спокойствие, баланс

514 319 893 714

Motivation
Motivation
Motivación
мотивация

49 87 14

Determination & Learning Focus
Détermination
Determinación
решимость, акцент на обучении

212 585 212

Determination
Détermination
Determinación
решимость

498 518 84 98

SLEEP
French: SOMMEIL
Spanish: SUEÑO
Russian: СОН

Sleep   148 542 321
Dormir
Dormir
Спать

Longer Sleep   754 14 34 11
Sommeil prolongé
Sueño prolongado
Продолжительный сон

Restful Sleep   54 11 23 21
Sommeil réparateur
Sueño reparador
Спокойный сон

Waking Up Feeling Refreshed   847 14 25 22
Se réveiller en se sentant rafraîchi
Despertarse sintiéndose renovad
Пробуждение с ощущением свежести

Eliminate Nightmares   72 44 11 531
Éliminer les cauchemars
Eliminar pesadillas
Устранение кошмаров

Improve Dreams Quality   343 234 211
Améliorer la qualité des rêves
Mejorar la calidad de los sueños
Улучшение качества сновидений

Dissolve Insomnia Issues   85 44 21 224
Dissoudre les problèmes d'insomnie
Disolver problemas de insomnio
Разрешение проблем с бессонницей

Help with falling asleep fast   544 543 21
Aide pour s'endormir rapidement
Ayuda para conciliar el sueño rápidamente
Помощь в быстром засыпании

Chronic Sleep Disorders and Fatigue   23 45 22 314
Troubles chroniques du sommeil et fatigue
Trastornos crónicos del sueño y fatiga
Хронические расстройства сна и усталость

To Prevent nightmare Anxiety and Worry 45 411 51 22
Prévenir l'anxiété et l'inquiétude des cauchemars
Prevenir la ansiedad y la preocupación de las pesadillas
Предотвращение тревоги и беспокойства от кошмаров

Sleep Quality
Qualité du sommeil
Calidad del sueño
Качество сна

98 414 22 52

Fall Asleep easier
S'endormir plus facilement
Conciliar el sueño más fácilmente
Легче засыпать

642 35 23 21

Invigorating Energy After Waking
Énergie revigorante après le réveil
Energía vigorizante después de despertar
Бодрящая энергия после пробуждения

1234 11 211

Reduces Anxiety
Réduit l'anxiété
Reduce la ansiedad
Снижение тревоги

897 491

Sleep Apnea
Apnée du sommeil
Apnea del sueño
Сонный апноэ

48 92 14 81948

TEETH
Teeth, Dents, Dientes, Зубы   **148 85 14**

Caries   514 85 84
Caries
Caries
Кариес

Health Tooth Cavities   586 20 43
Santé des cavités dentaires
Salud de las cavidades dentales
Здоровье зубных полостей

Teeth issues / Acute Pain   518 25 44
Problèmes dentaires / Douleur aiguë
Problemas dentales / Dolor agudo
Проблемы с зубами / Острая боль

Gingivitis   548 43 21 23
Gingivite
Gingivitis
Гингивит

Cavities eliminate   584
Éliminer les caries
Eliminar caries
Устранение кариеса

Periodontosis   581 45 42 1
Parodontose
Periodontosis
Периодонтоз

Tartar   51 48 5 21 82
Tartre
Tártaro
Зубной камень

Pulpitis
Pulpite
Pulpitis
Пульпит

146 85 50

Healthy Teeth and gums
Dents et gencives saines
Dientes y encías saludables
Здоровые зубы и десны

468 99 79 938

Stop Gums from Receding
Arrêter le recul des gencives
Detener la retracción de las encías
Остановить отступление десен

786 888 34 689

Teeth eliminate problem
Éliminer le problème dentaire
Eliminar el problema dental
Устранение зубной проблемы

98 477 84 66 89

Post Extraction Hemorrhage
Hémorragie post-extraction
Hemorragia post extracción
Кровотечение после экстракции

814 45 42

Toothe enamel
Émail dentaire
Esmalte dental
Зубная эмаль

618 374 898 161

Wisdom Tooth pain
Douleur de dent de sagesse
Dolor de muela del juicio
Боль мудрости зуба

893 66 106

Wisdom teeth   817 12 63
Dents de sagesse
Muelas del juicio
Зубы мудрости

To regenerate new teeth   268 060 785
Régénérer de nouvelles dents
Regenerar nuevos dientes
Регенерация новых зубов

Upper Molars   648 517 216 318
Molaires supérieures
Molares superiores
Верхние коренные зубы

Upper Minor Molars   694 317 219 498
Molaires supérieures mineures
Molares superiores menores
Верхние малые коренные зубы

Alveolar Process of Maxilla   986 149 318 518
Processus alvéolaire du maxillaire supérieur
Proceso alveolar del maxilar superior
Альвеолярный отросток верхней челюсти

Upper Incisors   519 671 918 549
Incisives supérieures
Incisivos superiores
Верхние резцы

Lower Lateral Incisors   989 718 514 601
Incisives latérales inférieures
Incisivos laterales inferiores
Нижние боковые резцы

Lower Central Incisors   584 716 914 219
Incisives centrales inférieures
Incisivos centrales medials
Нижние боковые резцы

Alveolar Part of Mandible (lower)   519 317 218 498
Partie alvéolaire de la mandibule (inférieure)
Parte alveolar de la mandíbula (inferior, arco inferior)
Альвеолярная часть нижней челюсти

Tooth Fracture   814 45 42 51
Fracture de la dent
Fractura del diente
Перелом зуба

Abscess in the Paranasal Sinuses   518 23 14 15
Abcès des sinus paranasaux
Absceso en los senos paranasales
Абсцесс околоносовых пазух

Teeth regrow   618 96 99
Repousse des dents
Regeneración dental
Регенерация зубов

Straight teeth   829 892 992
Dents droites
Dientes Rectos
Ровные зубы

EARS / Oreilles / Oídos / Уши   185 14 32

Otitis   551 84 321
Otite
Otitis
Отит

Ciliated Cells   512 418 622 898
Cellules ciliées
Células ciliadas
Ресничные клетки

Auditory Ossicles   428 317 218 227

English: Auditory Ossicles
French: Ossicules auditifs
Spanish: Ossículos auditivos
Russian: Слуховые косточки

Vestibulocochlear Nerve   219 314 218 712

English: Vestibulocochlear Nerve
French: Nerf vestibulocochléaire
Spanish: Nervio vestibulococlear
Russian: Вестибулокохлеарный нерв

Auditory and Vestibular System   248 712 318 222
English: Auditory and Vestibular System
French: Système auditif et vestibulaire
Spanish: Sistema auditivo y vestibular
Russian: Аудиторная и вестибулярная система

Tinnitus (ringing in the ear) **148 85 13**
Soulager les acouphènes (bourdonnements)
Aliviar el zumbido en el oído (tinnitus)
Облегчить звон в ушах (тиннитус)

Otosclerosis **481 48 51**
hearing impairment in young adults
French: Otosclérose
Spanish: Otosclerosis
Russian: Отосклероз

Otohematos **485 31 21**
English: Otohematos
French: Hématome de l'oreille, Otohématos
Spanish: Hematoma en el oído, Otohematos
Russian: Отогематос

Ear Trauma **45 48 515**
French: Traumatisme de l'oreille
Spanish: Trauma auditivo
Russian: Травма уха

Deafness **148 54 32 92**
English: Deafness
French: Surdité
Spanish: Sordera
Russian: Глухота

HEAD

Reverse white hair   498 1943 1947
Inverser les cheveux blancs
Revertir el cabello blanco
Восстановить естественный цвет волос

Increase IQ   589 61 43 1798
Augmenter le QI
Augmentar el CI
Увеличить уровень IQ

Telepathy   519 89 49 1848
Télépathie, Telepatía, Телепатия

Clairvoyance   818 88 49 49 21 67
Clairvoyance
Clarividencia
Ясновидение

Open 3rd eyes   88 44 242
Ouvrir le troisième œil
Abrir el tercer ojo
Открыть третий глаз

Improve memory   589 32 40
Améliorer la mémoire
Mejorar la memoria
Улучшить память

Increase intuition   35 98 6
Augmenter l'intuition
Aumentar la intuición
Усилить интуицию

VITAMINS

English: Vitamin Disease
Maladie liée aux vitamines
 Enfermedad por deficiencia de vitaminas
Заболевание, связанное с витаминами

Vitamin disease   123 895
Maladie liée aux vitamines
Enfermedad por deficiencia de vitaminas
Заболевание, связанное с витаминами

Deficiency Disease   545 12 34
Maladie par carence
Enfermedad por deficiencia
Заболевание из-за дефицита

A lack of vitamin   415 48 12
Manque de vitamine
Falta de vitamina
Недостаток витамина

Deficiency of Vitamin B1   12345 78
Carence en vitamine B1
Deficiencia de vitamina B1
Дефицит витамина B1

Lack of vitamin B2   148 54 21
Manque de vitamine B2
Falta de vitamina B2
Недостаток витамина B2

Vitamin C   414 12 55
Vitamine C
Vitamina C
Витамин C

Vitamin D   542 14 32
Vitamine D
Vitamina D
Витамин D

Vitamin K   48 45 414
Vitamine K
Vitamina K
Витамин K

Iron Deficiency   145 84 21
Carence en fer
Deficiencia de hierro
Дефицит железа

Colagene   589 649 594 31
Collagène
Colágeno
Коллаген

Serotonin   514 81 23
Sérotonine
Serotonina
Серотонин

Arthritis   891 42 01
Arthrite
Artritis
Артрит

BODY

Physical Healing Codes (generic)
Codes de guérison physique (générique)
Códigos de curación física (genéricos)
Коды физического исцеления (универсальные)

Restoring Health   888 84 88 88 8
Restaurer la santé
Restaurar la salud
Восстановление здоровья

Healing the body   918 948 181
Guérir le corps
Curar el cuerpo
Исцеление тела

Weight loss   534 21 68
Perte de poids
Pérdida de peso
Похудение

Weight loss and health   189 10 14
Perte de poids et santé
Pérdida de peso y salud
Похудение и здоровье

Good Health   808 45 700
Bonne santé
Buena salud
Хорошее здоровье

Flat Belly   69 7 70 62 58
Ventre plat
Vientre plano
Плоский живот

Dream Body   824 06 92
Corps de rêve
Cuerpo soñado
Идеальное тело

Increase Beauty   835 85 17
Augmenter la beauté
Aumentar la belleza
Увеличить красоту

Good Health   **808 45 700**

Fertility   322 63 60
Fertilité
Fertilidad
Фертильность

Quit Smoking   141 45 51
Arrêter de fumer
Dejar de fumar
Бросить курить

Skin problems   185 8 4321
Problèmes de peau
Problemas de piel
Проблемы с кожей

Teeth Problems   148 85 14
Problèmes dentaires
Problemas dentales
Зубные проблемы

Improve Memory   589 32 40
Améliorer la mémoire
Mejorar la memoria
Улучшить память

Menopause   485 15 48
Ménopause
Menopausa
менопауза

High Blood Pressure   8 145 432
Hypertension artérielle
Hipertensión arterial
Артериальная гипертензия

Instant Healing   19 751
Guérison instantanée
Curación instantánea
Мгновенное исцеление

Rheumatism   5 481 543
Rhumatisme
Reumatismo
Ревматизм

Influenza / Flu   4 814 212
Grippe
Gripe
Грипп

Water Energization (Water Memory)   719
Write near a water bottle left for 15 minutes
Dynamisation de l'eau
A écrire près d'une bouteille d'eau pendant 15 minutes
Dinamización del Agua
Escribir cerca de una botella de agua dejada durante 15 minutos
Динамизация Воды
(Написать рядом с бутылкой воды, оставленной на 15 минут)

BODY - Eyes (18 codes !)

Eyes Vision　　　　　　　　　　57 683 76 24 69
Vision des yeux
Visión ocular
Зрение глаз

Vision improvement　　　　　　29 37 853
Amélioration de la vision
Mejora de la visión
Улучшение зрения

Early cataract　　　　　　　　77 78 177
Cataracte précoce
Catarata temprana
Ранняя катаракта

Eyes illness　　　　　　　　　189 10 14
Maladie des yeux
Enfermadades de los ojos
болезни глаза

Conjunctivitis　　　　　　　　518 43 14
Conjonctivite
Conjuntivitis
конъюнктивит

Myopia　　　　　　　　　　　548 132 198
Myopie
Miopía
Миопия

Astigmatism　　　　　　　　　142 15 43
Astigmatisme
Astigmatismo
астигматизм

Strabismus   518 543 254
Strabisme
Estrabismo
Страбизм

Retinitis   548 45 12
Rétinite
Retinitis
Ретинит

Retinal Detachment   185 17 60
Décollement de la Rétine
Desprendimiento de Retina
Отслоение сетчатки

Hyperopia   518 99 88
Hypermétropie
Hipermetropía
Гиперметропия

Improves eyesight   210 250 300
Améliorer la vue
Mejora la vista
Улучшает зрение

Open the 3rd eyes (intuition)   88 1 88 1 88 1
Ouvrir le troisième œil (intuition)
Abrir el tercer ojo (intuición)
Открыть третий глаз (интуиция)

Eliminate Sty   514 85 42 49
Éliminer un orgelet
Eliminar un orzuelo
Устранить ячмень (глаза)

Chalazion (eyelid cyst)   514 85 82
Chalazion (kyste de la paupière)
Chalazión (quiste del párpado)
Халязион (киста века)

Ptosis (drooping upper eyelids)   185 43 121
Ptôse (chute des paupières supérieures)
Ptosis (caída de los párpados superiores)
Птоз (опущение верхних век)

Exophthalmos (bulging eyes)   545 43 11
Exophtalmie (yeux exorbités)
Exoftalmia (ojos saltones)
Экзофтальм (выпученные глаза)

Amblyopia (lazy eye)   18 99 99 9
Amblyopie (œil paresseux)
Ambliopía (ojo vago)
Амблиопия (ленивый глаз)

BODY - Digestive System

Obesity   42 67 465 87 25
Obésité
Obesidad
Ожирение

Nausea   83 33 889
Nausée
Náusea
Тошнота

Motion Sickness   83 41 783
Mal des transports
Mareo por movimiento
Укачивание

Hepatitis of viral Energy   87 47 988
Hépatite de l'énergie virale
Hepatitis de energía viral
Гепатит вирусной энергии

Hepatitis C   22 35 966
Hépatite C
Hepatitis C
Гепатит C

Cirrhosis of the liver   22 35 297
Cirrhose du foie
Cirrosis hepática
Цирроз печени

BODY Illness / Specific Health Conditions

First Aid   938 179
Premiers secours
Primeros auxilios
Первая помощь

Heart Attack   891 678
Crise cardiaque
Ataque cardíaco
Сердечный приступ

Tumor Disease   821 43 51
Maladie tumorale
Enfermedad tumoral
Опухолевое заболевание

Miocardis Infarctus   891 43 25
Infarctus du myocarde
Infarto de miocardio
Инфаркт миокарда

Coma   111 0 1 2
Coma
Coma
Koma

Shock   189 51 32
Choc
Choque
Шок

Respiratory issues   519 71 48
Problèmes respiratoires
Problemas respiratorios
Респираторные проблемы

Full Protection
Protection complète
Protección completa
Полная защита

918 775 89 81 81 8

Stop smoking
Arrêter de fumer
Dejar de fumar
Бросить курить

14 14 551

Baldness
Calvitie
Calvicie
Облысение

548 41 21

To lose weight (ideal weight)
Perdre du poids
Perder peso
Похудеть

481 24 12

To lose weight (only)
Perdre du poids
Perder peso
Похудеть

6 847 673 928

Lucid Dreams
Rêves Lucides
Sueños lúcidos
осознанные сны

621 066 285

Healing
Guérison
Curación
Исцеление

858 54 13 210

CANCER HEALING CODES / Codes de Guérison du Cancer
Códigos de Curación del Cáncer / Коды Исцеления Рака

Bladder cancer   891 23 459
Cancer de la vessie
Cáncer de vejiga
Рак мочевого пузыря

Cancer of the Salivary Gland   985 43 21
Cancer de la glande salivaire
Cáncer de la glándula salival
Рак слюнной железы

Cancer of the Breast   543 21 89
Cancer du sein
Cáncer de mama
Рак молочной железы

Skin Cancer   814 89 57
Cancer de la peau
Cáncer de piel
Рак кожи

Prostate Cancer   432 18 90
Cancer de la prostate
Cáncer de próstata
Рак простаты

Cancer in the thyroid –   581 45 42
Cancer de la thyroïde
Cáncer de tiroides
Рак щитовидной железы

Cancer of the gallbladder –
Cancer de la vésicule biliaire
Cáncer de vesícula biliar
Рак желчного пузыря

891 24 53

Cancer of the extrahepatic via gallbladder –
Cancer des voies biliaires extra-hépatiques
Cáncer de las vías biliares extrahepáticas
Рак внепеченочных желчных путей

578 91 54

Cancer in the vagina and external sex organs –
Cancer du vagin et des organes génitaux externes
Cáncer en la vagina y órganos sexuales externos
Рак влагалища и наружных половых органов

125 891 21

Cancer in the large duodenal papilla –
Cancer de la grande papille duodénale
Cáncer en la gran papila duodenal
Рак большой дуоденальной сосочки

891 23 45

Esophageal cancer –
Cancer de l'œsophage
Cáncer de esófago
Рак пищевода

891 25 67

Stomach cancer –
Cancer de l'estomac
Cáncer de estómago
Рак желудка

891 25 34

Liver cancer –
Cancer du foie
Cáncer de hígado
Рак печени

589 1248

Cancer in the large intestine (colon and rectum) – 5,821,435
Cancer du gros intestin (côlon et rectum)
Cáncer en el intestino grueso (colon y recto)
Рак толстой кишки (ободочной и прямой кишки)

Ovarian cancer –   485 19 23
Cancer de l'ovaire
Cáncer de ovario
Рак яичников

Pancreatic cancer –   812 58 91
Cancer du pancréas
Cáncer de páncreas
Рак поджелудочной железы

Cancer of the penis –   851 49 21
Cancer du pénis
Cáncer de pene
Рак полового члена

Kidney cancer –   567 89 108
Cancer du rein
Cáncer de riñón
Рак почек

Ureter cancer –   589 1856
Cancer de l'uretère
Cáncer del uréter
Рак мочеточника

Cancer on the lips –   156 78 12
Cancer des lèvres
Cáncer en los labios
Рак губ

Lymphoma in the skin –   589 12 43
Lymphome cutané
Linfoma en la piel
Лимфома кожи

Melanoma –   567 43 21
Mélanome
Melanoma
Меланома

Mesothelioma –   589 124 34
Mésothéliome
Mesotelioma
Мезотелиома

Neuroblastoma –   891 45 67
Neuroblastome
Neuroblastoma
Нейробластома

Rabdomy sarcoma in children –   567 12 54
Sarcome rhabdomyoïde chez les enfants
Sarcoma rabdomioide en niños
Рабдомиосаркома у детей

Kaposi sarcoma –   821 43 82
Sarcome de Kaposi
Sarcoma de Kaposi
Саркома Капоши

Soft tissue sarcoma –   54321891
Sarcome des tissus mous
Sarcoma de tejidos blandos
Саркома мягких тканей

Brain tumor (brain and spinal cord) – 5 431 547
Tumeur cérébrale (cerveau et moelle épinière)
Tumor cerebral (cerebro y médula espinal)
Опухоль головного мозга

Malignant tumor in the area of the mouth & throat 1235689
Tumeur maligne de la bouche et de la gorge
Tumor maligno en la boca y la garganta
Злокачественная опухоль в области рта и горла

Malignant tumor in the small intestine – 5485143
Tumeur maligne de l'intestin grêle
Tumor maligno en el intestino delgado
Злокачественная опухоль тонкой кишки

Malignant bone tumor – 1234589
Tumeur osseuse maligne
Tumor óseo maligno
Злокачественная костная опухоль

Malignant testicular tumors – 5814321
Tumeurs testiculaires malignes
Tumores testiculares malignos
Злокачественные опухоли яичек

Tumors in the nose and throat area – 5678910
Tumeurs dans la zone du nez et de la gorge
Tumores en la nariz y área de la garganta
Опухоли в области носа и горла

Tumors in parathyroid – 1548910
Tumeurs des parathyroïdes
Tumores en paratiroides
Опухоли паращитовидной железы

Tumors of the adrenal –   5678123
Tumeurs des glandes surrénales
Tumores de las glándulas suprarrenales
Опухоли надпочечников

Tumors in the nose and paranasal sinuses –   8514256
Tumeurs du nez et des sinus paranasaux
Tumores en la nariz y senos paranasales
Опухоли носа и околоносовых пазух

Tumors in the pancreas in Langerhans islands – 8951432
Tumeurs du pancréas dans les îlots de Langerhans
Tumores en el páncreas en las islas de Langerhans
Опухоли поджелудочной железы в островках Лангерганса

Tumors in the uterus   9817453
Tumeurs de l'utérus
Tumores en el útero
Опухоли матки

Sepsis Chapter   58,143,212
Chapitre sur la septicémie
Capítulo sobre la sepsis
Глава о сепсисе

Acute sepsis   891 43 21
Sepsis aigu
Sepsis aguda
Острый сепсис

Chronic sepsis   814 54 21
Sepsis chronique
Sepsis crónica
Хронический сепсис

DIC syndrome and wear coagulopathy –   514 81 42
Syndrome de CIVD et coagulopathie d'usure
Síndrome DIC y coagulopatía por desgaste
Синдром ДВС и износ коагулопатии

DIC syndrome   812 34 54
Syndrome de CIVD
Síndrome DIC
Синдром ДВС

Diseases of the circulatory system –   1,289,435
Maladies du système circulatoire
Enfermedades del sistema circulatorio
Заболевания сердечно-сосудистой системы

Abnormal heart rhythm –   854 32 10
Rythme cardiaque anormal
Ritmo cardíaco anormal
Ненормальный сердечный ритм

Aneurysm in the aorta –   485 432 18
Anévrisme de l'aorte
Aneurisma en la aorta
Аневризма аорты

Aneurysm of the heart –   918 75 49
Anévrisme du cœur
Aneurisma del corazón
Аневризма сердца

Angina pectoris (heart angina) –   8 145 999
Angine de poitrine
Angina de pecho
Стенокардия (грудная жаба)

Arteriosclerosis –   543 2 1898
Artériosclérose
Arteriosclerosis
Атеросклероз

Cardial asthma –   854 32 14
Asthme cardiaque
Asma cardíaca
Кардиальная астма

Coronary blockage –   987 43 21
Blocage coronarien
Bloqueo coronario
Коронарная блокада

Cardialgia –   812 45 67
Cardialgie
Cardialgia
Кардиалгия

Collapse (acute vascular insufficiency) –   8 914 320
Effondrement (insuffisance vasculaire aiguë)
Colapso (insuficiencia vascular aguda)
Коллапс (острая сосудистая недостаточность)

Cor pulmonale –   543 21 11
Cor pulmonaire
Cor pulmonale
Легочное сердце (кор пульмонале)

Circulatory crisis (pots) –   8,543,218
Crise circulatoire (pots)
Crisis circulatoria (pots)
Криз циркуляции крови (постуральный
ортостатический тахикардический синдром)

Hypertensive crisis –   567 91 02
Crise hypertensive
Crisis hipertensiva
Гипертонический криз

Neurocirculatório dystonia –   543 21 50
Dystonie neurocirculatoire
Dystonía neurocirculatoria
Нейроциркуляторная дистония

Vegetative dystonia vascular –   843 29 10
Dystonie végétative vasculaire
Dystonía vegetativa vascular
Вегетососудистая дистония

Myocardial dystrophy –   854 32 104
Dystrophie myocardique
Distrofia miocárdica
Миокардиальная дистрофия

Coronary heart disease caused by hypertension – 814 54 32
Maladie coronarienne causée par l'hypertension
Enfermedad coronaria causada por hipertensión
Коронарная болезнь сердца, вызванная гипертонией

Ischemic heart disease –   145 42 10
Maladie cardiaque ischémique
Enfermedad cardíaca isquémica
Ишемическая болезнь сердца

Pulmonary edema –   543 21 112
Œdème pulmonaire
Edema pulmonar
Легочный отек

Endocarditis –   854 54 21
Endocardite
Endocarditis
Эндокардит

Myocardial infarction (coronary) –   8 914 325
Infarctus du myocarde (coronaire)
Infarto de miocardio (coronario)
Инфаркт миокарда (коронарный)

Coronary sclerosis –   489 10 67
Sclérose coronarienne
Esclerosis coronaria
Коронарный склероз

Hypertension –   814 54 32
Hypertension
Hipertensión
Гипертония

Hypotension –   814 35 46
Hypotension
Hipotensión
Гипотония

Idiopathic myocardial –   843 21 42
Myocardique idiopathique
Miocárdico idiopático
Идиопатическая миокардиопатия

Circulatory failure –   854 32 102
Défaillance circulatoire
Insuficiencia circulatoria
Сердечно-сосудистая недостаточность

Coronary heart disease –   854 21 06
Maladie coronarienne
Enfermedad coronaria
Коронарная болезнь сердца

Vascular insufficiency –   866 8888
Insuffisance vasculaire
Insuficiencia vascular
Сосудистая недостаточность

Myocarditis –   843 21 10
Myocardite
Miocarditis
Миокардит

Cardiac myopathy –   842 143 2
Cardiomyopathie
Miocardiopatía
Кардиомиопатия

Arterial occlusion –   815 432 13
Occlusion artérielle
Oclusión arterial
Артериальная окклюзия

Pericarditis –   999 6 127
Péricardite
Pericarditis
Перикардит

Coronary problem acquired –   812 45 69
Problème coronarien acquis
Problema coronario adquirido
Приобретенная коронарная проблема

Congenital coronary problem –   999 54 37
Problème coronarien congénital
Problema coronario congénito
Врожденная коронарная проблема

Rheumatism –   548 15 43
Rhumatisme
Reumatismo
Ревматизм

Thrombophlebitis –   145 45 80
Thrombophlébite
Tromboflebitis
Тромбофлебит

Varicose (varices) –   4,831,388
Varices (veines variqueuses)
Varices
Варикозное расширение вен (варикоз)

Esophageal varices   25 36 591
Varices œsophagiennes
Varices esofágicas
Варикозное расширение вен пищевода

Systemic vasculitis –   189 42 38
Vascularite systémique
Vasculitis sistémica
Системный васкулит

Rheumatic Diseases –   8 148 888
Maladies rhumatismales
Enfermedades reumáticas
Ревматические заболевания

Takayasu arteritis (granulomatous vasculitis)   8 945 432
Artérite de Takayasu (vasculite granulomateuse)
Arteritis de Takayasu (vasculitis granulomatosa)
Артериит Такаясу (гранулематозный васкулит)

Temporal arteritis giant cell –   999 81 02
Artérite temporale à cellules géantes
Arteritis temporal de células gigantes
Гигантоклеточный артериит (артериит височной артерии)

Infectious arthritis –   811 11 10
Arthrite infectieuse
Artritis infecciosa
Инфекционный артрит

Arthritis (microcristaloide) –   0 014 235
Arthrite (microcristalloïde)
Artritis (microcristaloide)
Артрит (микрокристаллоидный)

Rheumatoid arthritis –   891 42 01
Polyarthrite rhumatoïde
Artritis reumatoide
Ревматоидный артрит

Arthropathy psoriatic –   01 45 421
Arthropathie psoriasique
Artropatía psoriásica
Псориатическая артропатия

Dermatomyositis (polymyositis) –   5,481,234
Dermatomyosite (polymyosite)
Dermatomiositis (polimiositis)
Дерматомиозит (полимиозит)

Diseases of the joints –   542 18 91
Maladies des articulations
Enfermedades de las articulaciones
Заболевания суставов

Diffuse connective tissue diseases –   548 58 12
Maladies du tissu conjonctif diffus
Enfermedades del tejido conectivo difuso
Диффузные заболевания соединительной ткани

Mixed connective tissue disease –   148 40 19
Maladie du tissu conjonctif mixte
Enfermedad del tejido conectivo mixto
Смешанная болезнь соединительной ткани

Rheumatic diseases   148 91 23
Maladies rhumatismales
Enfermedades reumáticas
Ревматические заболевания

Systemic Scleroderma –   111 00 06
Sclérodermie systémique
Esclerodermia sistémica
Системная склеродермия

Drop –   854 32 15
Goutte
Gota
Подагра

Granulomatosis (Wegener) –   8 943 568
Granulomatose (Wegener)
Granulomatosis (Wegener)
Гранулематоз (Вегенера)

Systemic lupus eridematoso –   85 431 48
Lupus érythémateux systémique
Lupus eritematoso sistémico
Системная красная волчанка

Deforming osteoarthritis –   81 45 812
Ostéoarthrite déformante
Osteoartritis deformante
Деформирующий остеоартрит

Periarthritis –   45 481 45
Périarthrite
Periartritis
Периартрит

Periarteritis nodosa –   543 218 94
Périartérite noueuse
Periarteritis nodosa
Периартериит узловатый

Rheumatism –   548 15 43
Rhumatisme
Reumatismo
Ревматизм

Bechterew syndrome (ankylosing spondylitis) –   4 891 201
Syndrome de Bechterew (spondylarthrite ankylosante)
Síndrome de Bechterew (espondilitis anquilosante)
Синдром Бехтерева (анкилоз

Goodpasture's syndrome
 (pulmonary purpura with nephritis) –   8 491 454
Syndrome de Goodpasture (purpura pulmonaire avec néphrite)
Síndrome de Goodpasture (púrpura pulmonar con nefritis)
Синдром Гудпасчера (пульмонарный пурпура с нефритом)

Reiter's syndrome (spondyloarthritis) –   4,848,111
Syndrome de Reiter (spondylarthrite)
Síndrome de Reiter (espondiloartritis)
Синдром Рейтера (спондилоартрит)

Sjögren's syndrome (progressive disease of the exocrine gland tissue system
autoimmune) –   489 14 56
Syndrome de Sjögren (maladie progressive du tissu glandulaire
exocrine auto-immune)
Síndrome de Sjögren (enfermedad progresiva del tejido de las
glándulas exocrinas autoinmune)
Синдром Шегрена (прогрессирующая болезнь экзокринной
железистой ткани аутоиммунная)

Tendovaginitis –   148 91 54
Tendovaginite
Tendovaginitis
Тендовагинит

Thromboangiitis obliterans –   894 54 82
Thromboangéite oblitérante
Tromboangeítis obliterante
Тромбоангиит облитерирующий

Hemorrhagic vasculitis –   849 12 34
Vascularite hémorragique
Vasculitis hemorrágica
Геморрагический васкулит

Systemic vasculitis –   189 42 38
Vascularite hémorragique
Vasculitis hemorrágica
Системный васкулит

Respiratory Diseases –   5,823,214
Maladies respiratoires
Enfermedades respiratorias
Заболевания органов дыхания

Anthracosis –   584 32 14
Anthracose
Antracosis
Антракоз

Asbestosis –   481 43 21
Asbestose
Asbestosis
Асбестоз

Bronchial asthma –
Asthme bronchique
Asma bronquial
Бронхиальная астма

894 35 48

Aspergillosis –
Aspergillose
Aspergilosis
Аспергиллез

481 543 271

Acute stomach atony –
Atonie gastrique aiguë
Atonía gástrica aguda
Острая атония желудка

548 56 71

Bronchiolitis –
Bronchiolite
Bronquiolitis
Бронхиолит

891 43 215

Acute bronchitis –
Bronchite aiguë
Bronquitis aguda
Острый бронхит

481 25 67

Chronic bronchitis –
Bronchite chronique
Bronquitis crónica
Хронический бронхит

421 89 10

Lung cancer –
Cancer du poumon
Cáncer de pulmón
Рак легкого

454 15 89

Candidiasis in the lung –
Candidose pulmonaire
Candidiasis en el pulmón
Кандидоз легких

489 14 44

Carboconiose –
Carboconiose
Carboconiosis
Карбокониоз

814 85 45

Pulmonary infarction –
Infarctus pulmonaire
Infarto pulmonar
Легочный инфаркт

891 432 11

Pulmonary emphysema –
Emphysème pulmonaire
Enfisema pulmonar
Эмфизема легких

543 21 892

Pulmonary sclerosis –
Sclérose pulmonaire
Esclerosis pulmonar
Склероз легких

987 12 34

Hepatic impairment –
Altération hépatique
Deterioro hepático
Печеночная недостаточность

814 32 14

Metaloconiose –
Métalloconiose
Metalconiosis
Металлокониоз

484 55 84

Chronic pancreatitis –
Pancréatite chronique
Pancreatitis crónica
Хронический панкреатит

589 14 32

Pleurisy –
Pleurésie
Pleuresía
Плеврит

485 4444

Stomach pneumatosis –
Pneumatose gastrique
Neumatosis estomacal
Газовая болезнь желудка (пневматоз желудка)

543 214 55

Pneumonia –
Pneumonie
Neumonía
Пневмония

481 44 89

Pneumoconiosis –
Pneumoconiose
Neumoconiosis
Пневмокониоз

842 34 57

Organic dust pneumoconiosis –
Pneumoconiose aux poussières organiques
Neumoconiosis por polvo orgánico
Пневмокониоз органической пыли

454 89 12

Sarcoidosis –
Sarcoïdose
Sarcoidosis
Саркоидоз

458 91 23

Silicatosis –
Silicatose
Silicatosis
Силикатоз

222 46 98

Silicosis –
Silicose
Silicosis
Силикоз

481 89 12

Hamann-Rich syndrome (alveolitis) –
Syndrome de Hamann-Rich (alvéolite)
Síndrome de Hamann-Rich (alveolitis)
Синдром Хамана-Рича (альвеолит)

4 814 578

Talcosis –
Talcose
Talcosis
Тальകоз

484 51 45

Pulmonary tuberculosis –
Tuberculose pulmonaire
Tuberculosis pulmonar
Туберкулез легких

894 12 34

Diseases of the digestive organs –
Maladies des organes digestifs
Enfermedades de los órganos digestivos
Заболевания органов пищеварения

532 14 82

Achalasia cardia –
Achalasie cardiaque
Acalasia cardíaca
Ахалазия кардии

489 51 23

Food allergy –   284 14 82
Allergie alimentaire
Alergia alimentaria
Пищевая аллергия

Amebiasis –   128 91 45
Amibiase
Amebiasis
Амебиаз

Amyloidosis –   543 21 85
Amylose
Amiloidosis
Амилоидоз

Functional stomach
Aquilia –   843 21 57
Aquilie (estomac fonctionnel)
Aquilia (estómago funcional)
Акилия (функциональный желудок)

Atony of the esophagus and stomach –   812 34 57
Atonie de l'œsophage et de l'estomac
Atonía del esófago y estómago
Атония пищевода и желудка

Bauhinite (inflammation of the ileocecal valve) –   58 432 148
Inflammation de la valvule de Bauhin (Bauhinite)
Inflamación de la válvula de Bauhin (Bauhinitis)
Воспаление клапана Баугина (Баугинит)

Beriberi –   348 91 12
Béribéri
Beriberi
Бери-бери

Bulbite –
Bulbite
Bulbitis
Бульбит

543 21 14

Candidiasis –
Candidose
Candidiasis
Кандидоз

548 421 48

Liver cirrhosis –
Cirrhose du foie
Cirrosis hepática
Цирроз печени

481 23 45

Pigmentary cirrhosis –
Cirrhose pigmentaire
Cirrosis pigmentaria
Пигментный цирроз

545 45 89

Acute cholecystitis –
Cholécystite aiguë
Colecistitis aguda
Острый холецистит

415 43 82

Chronic cholecystitis –
Cholécystite chronique
Colecistitis crónica
Хронический холецистит

548 12 45

Gallstones –
Calculs biliaires
Cálculos biliares
Желчные камни

014 80 12

Intestinal colic –
Colique intestinale
Cólico intestinal
Кишечная колика

812 34 57

Colitis –
Colite
Colitis
Колит

845 4 321

Acute colitis –
Colite aiguë
Colitis aguda
Острый колит

543 2145

Chronic colitis –
Colite chronique
Colitis crónica
Хронический колит

548 12 38

Constipation –
Constipation
Estreñimiento
Запор

548 45 48

Hepatoventricular degeneration –
Dégénérescence hépatoventriculaire
Degeneración hepatoventricular
Гепатовентрикулярная дегенерация

543 89 12

Diarrhea –
Diarrhée
Diarrea
Диарея

584 32 18

Functional diarrhea –　　　　　812 345 74
Diarrhée fonctionnelle
Diarrea funcional
Функциональная диарея

Intestinal Dysbacteriosis –　　　543 21 01
Dysbactériose intestinale
Disbacteriosis intestinal
Кишечный дисбактериоз

Biliary dyskinesia –　　　　　　584 32 144
Dyskinésie biliaire
Discinesia biliar
Дискинезия желчевыводящих путей

Dyskinesia bowel –　　　　　　543 21 893
Dyskinésie intestinale
Discinesia intestinal
Дискинезия кишечника

Dyskinesia of the intestinal tract (motor functional alteration of the intestine) –　　　　　8 123 457
Dyskinésie du tractus intestinal (altération fonctionnelle motrice de l'intestin)
Discinesia del tracto intestinal (alteración funcional motora del intestino)
Дискинезия кишечного тракта
(функциональное моторное нарушение кишечника)

Spastic esophageal dyskinesia –　　548 12 48
Dyskinésie œsophagienne spastique
Discinesia esofágica espástica
Спастическая дискинезия пищевода

Dyspepsia –　　　　　　　　　111 22 23
Dyspepsie
Dispepsia
Диспепсия

Food dystrophy –   545 67 84
Dystrophie alimentaire
Distrofia alimentaria
Пищевая дистрофия

Liver dystrophy –   987 65 12
Dystrophie hépatique
Distrofia hepática
Печеночная дистрофия

Uipl disease (intestinal lipodystrophy) –   4 814 548
Maladie de Uipl (lipodystrophie intestinale)
Enfermedad de Uipl (lipodistrofia intestinal)
Болезнь Уипла (кишечная липодистрофия)

Duodenitis –   543 21 14
Duodénite
Duodenitis
Дуоденит

Acute duodenitis –   481 543 288
Duodénite aiguë
Duodenitis aguda
Острый дуоденит

Chronic duodenitis –   843 21 54
Duodénite chronique
Duodenitis crónica
Хронический дуоденит

Duodenostase –   812 34 57
Duodénostase
Duodenostasis
Дуоденостаз

Enteritis –
Entérite
Enteritis
Энтерит

843 12 87

Acute enteritis –
Entérite aiguë
Enteritis aguda
Острый энтерит

543 21 481

Chronic enteritis –
Entérite chronique
Enteritis crónica
Хронический энтерит

543 21 40

Enterocolitis –
Entérocolite
Enterocolitis
Энтероколит

845 43 21

Caused by gluten enteropathy –
Entéropathie causée par le gluten
Enteropatía causada por gluten
Энтеропатия, вызванная глютеном

489 14 83

Exudative enteropathy –
Entéropathie exsudative
Enteropatía exudativa
Экссудативная энтеропатия

481 234 54

Enteropathy (lymphangiectasis) intestinal
Entéropathie intestinale (lymphangiectasie)
Enteropatía intestinal (linfangiectasia)
Кишечная энтеропатия (лимфангиэктазия)

521 4321

Intestinal enteropathy –
Entéropathie intestinale
Enteropatía intestinal
Кишечная энтеропатия

843 2150

Enteropathy deficit disaccharidase –
Entéropathie à déficit en disaccharidase
Enteropatía por déficit de disacaridasa
Энтеропатия с дефицитом дисахаридазы

484 5432

Scurvy –
Scorbut
Escorbuto
Цинга

543 2190

Esophagitis –
Œsophagite
Esofagitis
Эзофагит

543 21 489

Spasm in the cardia –
Spasme du cardia
Espasmo en la cardias
Спазм кардии

489 5132

Spasm in the esophagus –
Spasme de l'œsophage
Espasmo en el esófago
Спазм пищевода

812 3457

Fleimões (popular flegmões) stomach –
Phlegmons (fleimões) de l'estomac
Flemón (fleimões) del estómago
Флегмона (флемон) желудка

456 7891

Gastritis –   548 5674
Gastrite
Gastritis
Гастрит

Acute gastritis –   456 7891
Gastrite aiguë
Gastritis aguda
Острый гастрит

Chronic gastritis –   548 9120
Gastrite chronique
Gastritis crónica
Хронический гастрит

Gastroenteritis –   548 5674
Gastro-entérite
Gastroenteritis
Гастроэнтерит

Gastroenterocolitis –   843 1287
Gastro-entérocolite
Gastroenterocolitis
Гастроэнтероколит

Gastroptosis –   812 34574
Gastroptose
Gastroptosis
Гастроптоз

Fat in the liver (fatty liver) –   143 214
Graisse dans le foie (foie gras)
Grasa en el hígado (hígado graso)
Жир в печени (жировой гепатоз)

Hemochromatosis (diabetes with iron deposits in the pancreas) – 5 454 589
Hémochromatose (diabète avec dépôts de fer dans le pancréas)
Hemocromatosis (diabetes con depósitos de hierro en el páncreas)
Гемохроматоз (диабет с отложением железа в поджелудочной железе)

Hepatitis –   581 4243
Hépatite
Hepatitis
Гепатит

Acute hepatitis –   584 32141
Hépatite aiguë
Hepatitis aguda
Острый гепатит

Functional hepatitis (jaundice, hiperbilirumenia) –   84 514 851
Hépatite fonctionnelle (jaunisse, hyperbilirubinémie)
Hepatitis funcional (ictericia, hiperbilirrubinemia)
Функциональный гепатит (желтуха, гипербилирубинемия)

Acute viral hepatitis (may be caused by *Hepatitis A, B, Salmonella*,
leptospirosis, and other enteroviruses) –   584 321 41
Hépatite virale aiguë (peut être causée par l'hépatite A, B, la salmonelle,
la leptospirose et d'autres entérovirus)
Hepatitis viral aguda (puede ser causada por Hepatitis A, B, Salmonella,
leptospirosis y otros enterovirus)
Острый вирусный гепатит (может быть вызван гепатитом А, В,
сальмонеллой, лептоспирозом и другими энтеровирусами)

Chronic hepatitis –   512 38 91
Hépatite chronique
Hepatitis crónica
Хронический гепатит

Hepatose –
Hépatose
Hepatosis
Гепатоз

987 65 12

Acute Hepatose –
Hépatose aiguë
Hepatosis aguda
Острый гепатоз

123 45 76

Hepatose cholestatic –
Hépatose cholestatique
Hepatosis colestásica
Холестатический гепатоз

542 15 48

Essential hyperlipidemia –
Hyperlipidémie essentielle
Hiperlipidemia esencial
Эссенциальная гиперлипидемия

485 18 88

Functional stomach hypersecretion –
Hyper sécrétion gastrique fonctionnelle
Hipersecreción gástrica funcional
Функциональная гиперсекреция желудка

548 42 14

Portal vein hypertension –
Hypertension de la veine porte
Hipertensión de la vena porta
Гипертензия воротной вены

814 32 18

Congenital functional hyperbilirubinemia –
Hyperbilirubinémie fonctionnelle congénitale
Hiperbilirrubinemia funcional congénita
Врожденная функциональная гипербилирубинемия

843 21 80

Post-hepatic hyperbilirubinemia –   821 43 21
Hyperbilirubinémie post-hépatique
Hiperbilirrubinemia post-hepática
Постгепатическая гипербилирубинемия

Hypovitaminosis –   515 4321
Hypovitaminose
Hipovitaminosis
Гиповитаминоз

Jaundice –   543 2148
Jaunisse
Ictericia
Желтуха

Ileitis –   843 1287
Iléite
Ileitis
Илеит

Cardiac insufficiency –   854 5142
Insuffisance cardiaque
Insuficiencia cardíaca
Сердечная недостаточность

Intestinal lipodystrophy –   481 4548
Lipodystrophie intestinale
Lipodistrofia intestinal
Кишечная липодистрофия

Lipoidosis in hepatosplenomegaly –   485 1888
Lipoidose dans l'hépatosplénomégalie
Lipoidosis en hepatosplenomegalia
Липоидоз при гепатоспленомегалии

Jejunitis –   843 1287
Jéjunité
Yejunitis
Жеженит

Mesenteric arteriovenous occlusion (incomplete)   **5 891 234**
Occlusion artérioveineuse mésentérique (incomplète)
Oclusión arteriovenosa mesentérica (incompleta)
Неполная мезентериальная артериовенозная окклюзия

Gastrocardial syndrome (achalasia) –   5 458 914
Syndrome gastrocardiaque (achalasie)
Síndrome gastrocardíaco (acalasia)
Гастрокардиальный синдром (ахалазия)

Carcinoid syndrome –   484 81 45
Syndrome carcinoïde
Síndrome carcinoide
Карциноидный синдром

Maldigestion syndrome –   **99 88 771**
Syndrome de mal digestion
Síndrome de mal digestión
Синдром малопереваривания

Malabsorption syndrome –   4854 3215
Syndrome de malabsorption
Síndrome de malabsorción
Синдром мальабсорбции

Hepatolienal syndrome –   84 51 485
Syndrome hépatolienal
Síndrome hepatolienal
Гепатолиенальный синдром

Post-hepatic syndrome –   48 12 819
Sprue not tropical (intestinal enteropathy on sensitivity to gluten)
Syndrome post-hépatique
Síndrome post-hepático
Постгепатический синдром

Tropical sprue (tropical diarrhea)   5 481 215
Sprue tropical (diarrhée tropicale)
Sprue tropical (diarrea tropical)
Тропический спру (тропическая диарея)

Tuberculosis of the stomach-intestinal tract –   814 3215
Tuberculose du tractus gastro-intestinal
Tuberculosis del tracto gastrointestinal
Туберкулез желудочно-кишечного тракта

Gastroduodenal ulcer –   812 5432
Ulcère gastroduodénal
Úlcera gastroduodenal
Гастродуоденальная язва

Symptomatic ulcer stomach –   9671428
Ulcère d'estomac symptomatique
Úlcera estomacal sintomática
Симптоматическая язва желудка

Peptic ulcer of the esophagus –   843 2182
Ulcère peptique de l'œsophage
Úlcera péptica del esófago
Пептическая язва пищевода

Simple ulcer in the small intestine –
Ulcère simple de l'intestin grêle
Úlcera simple en el intestino delgado
Простая язва тонкой кишки

484 81452

Diseases of the kidney and urinary tract –
Maladies du rein et des voies urinaires
Enfermedades del riñón y del tracto urinario
Заболевания почек и мочевыводящих путей

894 1254

Amyloidosis –
Amyloïdose
Amiloidosis
Амилоидоз

451 2345

Abnormalities of the urinary tract –
Anomalies des voies urinaires
Anomalías del tracto urinario
Аномалии мочевыводящих путей

1 234 571

Cystitis –
Cystite
Cistitis
Цистит

485 43211

Multiple cysts in the kidneys –
Multiples kystes dans les reins
Múltiples quistes en los riñones
Множественные кисты в почках

542 1451

Renal colic –
Colique néphrétique
Cólico renal
Почечная колика

432 1054

Renal eclampsia –
Éclampsie rénale
Eclampsia renal
Почечная эклампсия

814 9141

Glomerulonephritis –
Glomérulonéphrite
Glomerulonefritis
Гломерулонефрит

481 2351

Acute glomerulonephritis –
Glomérulonéphrite aiguë
Glomerulonefritis aguda
Острый гломерулонефрит

428 5614

Hydronephrosis –
Hydronéphrose
Hidronefrosis
Гидронефроз

543 2154

Renal failure –
Insuffisance rénale
Insuficiencia renal
Почечная недостаточность

432 1843

Acute renal failure –
Insuffisance rénale aiguë
Insuficiencia renal aguda
Острая почечная недостаточность

821 8882

Chronic renal failure –   548 8821
Insuffisance rénale chronique
Insuficiencia renal crónica
Хроническая почечная недостаточность

Pyelitis –   543 2110
Pyélite
Pielitis
Пиелит

Pyelonephritis –   581 43213
Pyélonéphrite
Pielonefritis
Пиелонефрит

Renal tuberculosis –   5814543
Tuberculose rénale
Tuberculosis renal
Почечный туберкулез

Uremia –   542 18 22
Urémie
Uremia
Уремия

Chronic uremia –   8914381
Urémie chronique
Uremia crónica
Хроническая уремия

Urolithiasis –   543 2143
Urolithiase
Urolitiasis
Уролитиаз

Hematologic Diseases –   1 843 214

Maladies hématologiques
Enfermedades hematológicas
Гематологические заболевания

Agranulocytosis –   485 6742

Agranulocytose
Agranulocitosis
Агранулоцитоз

Anemia –   48 54 32 12

Anémie
Anemia
Анемия

Aplastic anemia (hypoplastic) –   5 481 541

Anémie aplastique (hypoplastique)
Anemia aplásica (hipoplásica)
Апластическая (гипопластическая) анемия

Anemia caused by poisoning and lead –   123 7819

Anémie causée par un empoisonnement et le plomb
Anemia causada por envenenamiento y plomo
Анемия, вызванная отравлением и свинцом

Anemia caused by megaloblasts –   548 1254

Anémie causée par les mégablastes
Anemia causada por megaloblastos
Мегалобластная анемия

Congenital anemia (anemia sideroacréstica) –   4 581 254

Anémie congénitale (anémie sidéroacréstique)
Anemia congénita (anemia sideroacréstica)
Врожденная анемия (сидероахрестическая анемия)

Hemolytic anemia –   548 4813
Anémie hémolytique
Anemia hemolítica
Гемолитическая анемия

Autoimmune hemolytic anemia –   581 4311
Anémie hémolytique auto-immune
Anemia hemolítica autoinmune
Аутоиммунная гемолитическая анемия

Acute post-hemorrhagic anemia –   948 1232
Anémie post-hémorragique aiguë
Anemia post-hemorrágica aguda
Острая постгеморрагическая анемия

Bleeding diathesis –   514 8543
Diathèse hémorragique
Diátesis hemorrágica
Геморрагический диатез

Vascular bleeding diathesis –   548 15438
Diathèse hémorragique vasculaire
Diátesis hemorrágica vascular
Сосудистый геморрагический диатез

Disprotrombinemia –   548 1542
Disprotrombinémie
Disprotrombinemia
Диспротромбинемия

Acute disease caused by radiation –   481 543 294
Maladie aiguë causée par les radiations
Enfermedad aguda causada por radiación
Острое заболевание, вызванное радиацией

Cytostatic disease –   4812813
Maladie cytostatique
Enfermedad citostática
Цитостатическая болезнь

Chronic disease caused by radiation –   4812453
Maladie chronique causée par les radiations
Enfermedad crónica causada por radiación
Хроническое заболевание, вызванное радиацией

Gaucher disease
(querasino reticular – cerebrosidlipoidose) –   5 145 432
Maladie de Gaucher (querasino réticulaire – cerebrosidlipoidose)
Enfermedad de Gaucher (querasino reticular – cerebrosidlipidosis)
Болезнь Гоше (керазино ретикулярное – цереброзидлипоидоз)

Favism –   543 214 57
Favisme
Favismo
Фавизм

Extramedullary hemoblastosis (lymphocytoma) – 54 321 451
Hémoblastose extramédullaire (lymphocytome)
Hemoblastosis extramedular (linfocitoma)
Внемозговая гемобластоза (лимфоцитома)

Hemoblastosis paraproteinêmica
(tumors in the lymphatic system)   8 432 184
Hémoblastose paraprotéinémique (tumeurs du système lymphatique)
Hemoblastosis paraproteinémica (tumores en el sistema linfático)
Парапротеинемическая гемобластоза (опухоли лимфатической системы)

Hemoglobinopathy –   789 1017
Hémoglobinopathie
Hemoglobinopatía
Гемоглобинопатия

Nocturnal hemoglobinuria paroximal –   548 1455
Hémoglobinurie nocturne paroxystique
Hemoglobinuria paroxística nocturna
Пароксизмальная ночная гемоглобинурия

Leukemia –   548 1347
Leucémie
Leucemia
Лейкемия

Lymphogranulomatosis –   484 5714
Lymphogranulomatose
Linfogranulomatosis
Лимфогранулематоз

Mielemia –   514 2357
Myélémie
Mielemia
Миелемия

SOUL & EMOTIONS

598 061 29131988

Charism
Charisme
Carisma
Харизма

491 718 594. 817

Clean E Memory
Nettoyer la mémoire électronique (*E Memory*)
Limpiar la memoria electrónica (*E Memory*)
Очистить электронную память (*E Memory*)

61 988 184 161

Fear
Peur
Miedo
Страх

489 712 819 48

Inside Peace
Paix intérieure
Paz interior
Внутренний мир

100 110 50 10

Joy
Joie
Alegria
Радость (Radost)

514 18 123

Depression
Dépression
Depresión
Депрессия

519 514 319 91

Agoraphobia
Agoraphobie
Agorafobia
Агорафобия

909 841 319 80 49

Turn negative into positive -
Transformer le négatif en positif
Convertir lo negativo en positivo
Превратить негатив в позитив

188 8 948

Connection with the creator
Connection avec le créateur
Conexión con el creado
Связь с творцом

123 70 44

Normalization of all chakras
Normalisation des chakras et des méridiens

8888 9 8888 7 8888

SACRED HEALING

I am divinely protected and shielded from all gossip and scandal.
305 980 101

Je suis divinement protégé et préservé de tous les commérages et scandales.
Estoy divinamente protegido y resguardado de todo chisme y escándalo.
Я божественно защищен и защищен от всех сплетен и скандалов.

Right now, we are immediately immune, protected, and shielded
<u>from all magic directed against us</u>   **313 255 288**

Dès maintenant, nous sommes immédiatement immunisés, protégés et à l'abri de toute magie dirigée contre nous.
En este momento, estamos inmediatamente inmunes, protegidos y resguardados de toda magia dirigida contra nosotros.
Прямо сейчас мы немедленно иммунизированы, защищены и укрыты от всякой магии, направленной против нас.

Protection from Energy Vampire   **148 55 144 52 183**
Protection contre les Vampires Énergétiques
Protección contra el Vampiro Energético
Защита от Энергетического Вампира

Open 3rd eye   **88 44 212**
Ouvrir 3ème oeil
Abrir tercero ojo
третий глаз

Healing Energy   **514 891**
Énergie de guérison
Energía de curación
Исцеляющая энергия (Istselayushchaya energiya)

MONEY ATTRACTION & ABUNDANCE (34 codes !)

Financial Abundance
Attraction de l'argent
Atracción de dinero
Привлечение денег

318 798

Resolve financial problems
Résoudre les problèmes financiers
Resolver problemas financieros
Решение финансовых проблем

137 421 33 99 14

Unexpected Money
Argent inattendu
Dinero inesperado
Неожиданные деньги

520 741 8

Unexpected Wealth
Richesse inattendue
Riqueza inesperada
Неожиданное богатство

175 170 38

Attract Money Fast
Attirer l'argent rapidement
Atraer dinero rápidamente
Быстро привлечь деньги

372 622 777

Money in your bank
Argent dans votre banque
Dinero en tu banco
Деньги в вашем банке

319 6 187 19 814

Flow of Money
Flux d'argent
Flujo de dinero
Поток денег

42 64 99

Achieve Goals
Atteindre des objectifs
Alcanzar objetivos
Достичь целей

894 719 78 48

Income and Business Success
Revenu et succès en affaires
Ingresos y éxito empresarial
Доход и успех в бизнесе

921 31 40

Entrepreneurship
Entrepreneuriat
Emprendimiento
Предпринимательство

719 741 12 19 81

Determination
Détermination
Determinación
Решимость

498 518 84 98

Money Confidence
Confiance en l'argent
Confianza en el dinero
Уверенность в деньгах

874 678 94

A Lot of Money
Beaucoup d'argent
Mucho dinero
Много денег

318 612 518 714

Unemployment
Chômage
Desempleo
Безработица

318 514 517 618

Money
Argent / Dinero / Деньги

964 91 30

Win for lottery
Gagner à la loterie
Ganar en la lotería
Выигрыш в лотерею

461 05 67

Money Magnet
Aimant à argent
Imán de dinero
Магнит для денег

199 62 1147

Professional Development
Développement Professionnel
Desarrollo Profesional
Профессиональное Развитие

138

Quick Money Switch words
Mots de commutation pour l'argent rapide
Palabras de cambio para dinero rápido
Быстрые слова-переключатели для денег

919 793

Becoming a Millionaire
Devenir millionnaire
Convertirse en millonario
Стать миллионером

71 42 27 32 1893

Everything is Possible
Tout est possible
Todo es posible
Всё возможно

519 71 48

Prosperity
Prospérité
Prosperidad
Процветание

714 27 32 18 93

Transformation of Time into Money
Transformation du temps en argent
Transformación del Tiempo en Dinero
Преобразование времени в деньги

414 81 88

Unlimited Money
Argent illimité
Dinero ilimitado
Неограниченные деньги

732 00 180

Money to Pay Bills
Argent pour payer les factures
Dinero para pagar facturas
Деньги на оплату счетов

69 75 01

Money Now
Argent maintenant
Dinero ahora
Деньги сейчас

72 99 99

Generate profits
Générer des profits
Generar beneficios
Генерировать прибыль

219 816

Financial Security
Sécurité Financière
Seguridad Financiera
Финансовая Безопасность

13 24 686 9789 4516

Prosperity and Wealth   536 389 589
Prospérité et Santé
Prosperidad y Riqueza
Процветание и Богатство

Harmonization of the Future   148 721 091
Harmonisation de l'Avenir
Armonización del Futuro
Гармонизация Будущего

Global Harmonization   918 794 48 181
Harmonisation Globale
Armonización Global
Глобальная Гармонизация

Space Purification   98 77 14 21 73
Purification de l'Espace
Purificación del Espacio
Очищение Пространства

Financial Success   819 47 11
Réussite Financière
Éxito Financiero
Финансовый Успех

Abundance + Wealth   520 318 798
Abondance + Richesse
Abundancia + Riqueza
Изобилие + Богатство (Izobilie + Bogatstvo)

Illness
Maladie
Enfermedad
Болезнь

Eyes problems   520 7418
Problèmes oculaires
Problemas oculares
Проблемы с глазами

Coronavirus   557 46 21
Coronavirus
Coronavirus
Коронавирус

Healing Coronavirus   877 489 73
Guérison du coronavirus
Curación del coronavirus
Излечение от коронавируса

Psoriasis   999 89 9181
Psoriasis
Psoriasis
Псориаз

Eczema   548 132 151
Eczéma
Eczema
Экзема

Headaches   481 8 543
Céphalées
Dolor de cabeza
Головные боли

Migraines (hémicrania)   483 1 421
Migraines (maux de têtes forts)
Migrañas (hemicránea)
Мигрень (гемикрания)

Tissue injury (mechanical lesion with rupture)   514 89 12
Blessure des tissus (lésion mécanique avec rupture) :
Lesión de tejidos (lesión mecánica con ruptura)
Повреждение тканей (механическое повреждение с разрывом

Contusion (mechanical lesion without rupture)   01 56 912
Contusion (lésion mécanique sans rupture)
Contusión (lesión mecánica sin ruptura)
Контузия (механическое повреждение без разрыва)

Glaucoma   513 14 82
Glaucome
Glaucoma
Глаукома

Carie dentaire / Teeth   514 8584
Carie dentaire / Dents
Caries dental / Dientes
Зубной кариес / Зубы

Sleeping challenge   514 24 8538
Trouble du sommeil
Problema de sueño
Проблемы со сном

Sprain   514 85 17
Entorse
Esguince
Растяжение

Laryngitis   454 8511
Laryngite
Laringitis
Ларингит

Diabetis   485 1421
Diabète sucré
Diabetes mellitus
Сахарный диабет

Flu   518 99 12
Rhume / Grippe
Resfriado / Gripe
Простуда / Грипп

Sinusitis   180 0124
Sinusite
Sinusitis
Синусит

Nervous Illness   148 543293
Maladie nerveuse
Enfermedad nerviosa
Нервное заболевание

Flu illness   58 23 21 4
Maladie de la grippe
Enfermedad de la gripe
Гриппозное заболевание

Common cold   48 14 212
Rhume commun
Resfriado común
Обычная простуда

Relieve cough   11 72 844
Soulager la toux
Aliviar la tos
Облегчить кашель

Release Alzheimer's Symptoms   481 854 383
Libérer des Symptômes d'Alzheimer
Liberar los Síntomas del Alzheimer
Облегчение Симптомов Болезни Альцгеймера

Relieve Parkinson's Disease   548 114 21
Soulager la Maladie de Parkinson
Aliviar la Enfermedad de Parkinson
Облегчение Болезни Паркинсона

Neurological Diseases   148 543 293
Maladies Neurologiques
Enfermedades Neurológicas
Неврологические Заболевания

Eternal Life   22 13 445
Vie éternelle
Vida eterna
Вечная жизнь

Rejuvenation for eternal growth 514
Rajeunissement pour une croissance éternelle
ejuvenecimiento para un crecimiento eterno
Омоложение для вечного роста

Regeneration of Brain Cells 518 43 213
Régénération des cellules cérébrales
Regeneración de células cerebrales
Регенерация мозговых клеток

Self Healing Body 918 79 48 181
Corps auto-guérisseur
Cuerpo autoregenerativo
Самовосстанавливающееся тело

Relieve sore Throat 1 999 999
Soulager le mal de gorge
Aliviar el dolor de garganta
Облегчить боль в горле

Strenghten your immune system 33 79 44 003
Renforcez votre système immunitaire
Forcatelece tu sistema immunologico
Укрепите вашу иммунную систему

Collagen ¨58 96 49 431
Collagène
Colageno
Коллаген

Problems of the spine and neck 548 13 21
Problème de colonnes et de nuque
Problemas de columna y cuello
Проблемы со спиной и шеей

Vertebral column
Colonne vertébrale
Columna vertebral
Позвоночник

214 217 000 819

Scoliose
Scoliose
Escoliosis
Сколиоз

43 52 45 855 84

Tendinitis (knees)
Tendinite
Tendinitis
Тендинит

148 91 54

Bursitis (elbow)
Bursite
Bursitis
Бурсит

751 84 321

Joint pain relief
Soulagement des douleurs articulaires
Alivio del dolor articular
Облегчение боли в суставах

512 18 91

Skin Diseases
Maladies de la peau
Enfermedades de la piel
Кожные заболевания

185 84 321

Against Respiratory Allergies
Contre les allergies respiratoires
Contra las alergias respiratorias
Против респираторных аллергий

415 43 212

LOWERING CHOLESTEROL *(exclusive codes !)*

Lowering Cholesterol between 30 - 39 years   **182 12 51**
Réduire le cholestérol entre 30 et 39 ans
Reducir el colesterol entre 30 y 39 años
Снижение холестерина в возрасте от 30 до 39 лет

Lowering Cholesterol between 40 - 49 years   **543 21 88 91**
Réduire le cholestérol entre 40 et 49 ans
Reducir el colesterol entre 40 y 49 años
Снижение холестерина в возрасте от 40 до 49 лет

Lowering Cholesterol between 50 - 59 years   **148 91 00**
Réduire le cholestérol entre 50 et 59 ans
Reducir el colesterol entre 50 y 59 años
Снижение холестерина в возрасте от 50 до 59 лет

Lowering Cholesterol between 60 - 69 years   **00 18 914**
Réduire le cholestérol entre 60 et 69 ans
Reducir el colesterol entre 60 y 69 años
Снижение холестерина в возрасте от 60 до 69 лет

Lowering Cholesterol people over 70 years old   **00 10 101**
Réduire le cholestérol chez les personnes de plus de 70 ans
Reducir el colesterol en personas mayores de 70 años
Снижение холестерина у людей старше 70 лет

Each **Grabovoi** number is a _beacon of healing_, a call to heal for the collective consciousness and your own healing (**710 42 Harmonization of the Present**) . From the heart of communities to the expanse of the globe, these numbers are the silent whispers of change, the invisible hands shaping a future where harmony, peace, and environmental stewardship are not just ideals, but realities.

In the realm of **Grabovoi** numbers, we're reminded that each of us plays a part in this symphony of **global healing**. Each number sequence is an instrument, and when played with intention and belief, they create a melody that resonates across the world, touching hearts, minds, and the very soul of our planet. You can heal and improve your well-being with these numbers , to recite it **unit by unit** once you've memorized it, feel it:

JOY   28 77 41

- Anglais: Joy 287741
- Français: Joie
- Espagnol: Alegría
- Russe: Радость

FREEDOM   514 89 47 19

- Anglais: Freedom 514894719
- Français: Liberté
- Espagnol: Libertad
- Russe: Свобода

OPTIMISM   498 917 18 19 48

- Anglais: Optimism 498917181948
- Français: Optimisme
- Espagnol: Optimismo
- Russe: Оптимизм

WILL POWER   513 96 48 18 91

- Anglais: Willpower 51396481891
- Français: Volonté
- Espagnol: Voluntad
- Russe: Воля

SELF CONFIDENCE   517 48 97 19 841

- Anglais: Self-confidence 517489719841
- Français: Confiance en soi
- Espagnol: Confianza en sí mismo
- Russe: Уверенность в себе

EMOTIONAL CALM   100 110 50 10

- Anglais: Emotional Calm 1001105010
- Français: Calme émotionnel
- Espagnol: Calma emocional
- Russe: Эмоциональное спокойствие

ENERGY AND VITALITY   189 10 13

- Anglais: Energy and Vitality 1891013
- Français: Tonus et vitalité
- Espagnol: Tono y vitalidad
- Russe: Тонус и жизненная энергия

COMBAT STRESS   819 471

- Anglais: Combat Stress 819471
- Français: Lutter contre le stress
- Espagnol: Combatir el estrés
- Russe: Борьба со стрессом

ELIMINATE GUILT 239 401 91 96 71

- Anglais: Eliminate Guilt 239401919671
- Français: Faire disparaître la culpabilité
- Espagnol: Eliminar la culpa
- Russe: Избавление от вины

OVERCOME ANXIETY ATTACK 548 571 21 918

- Anglais: Overcome Anxiety Attack 548 571 21 918
- Français: Vaincre une crise d'angoisse
- Espagnol: Superar una crisis de ansiedad
- Russe: Преодоление приступа тревоги

HARMONIZE OF ALL CHAKRAS 8888 9 8888 78 888

- Anglais: Harmonize of all chakras 8888 9 8888 78 888
- Français: Harmonisation de tous les Chakras
- Espagnol: Armonizacion de todos los Chakras
- Russe: Гармонизация всех чакр

CANCEL THE KARMA 791

- Anglais: Cancel the Karma
- Français: Annuler le Karma
- Espagnol: Cancelar el Karma
- Russe: Отменить Карму

Continuing our journey with the whimsical charm and wit of our literary guides, Chapter 6 of our book on **Grabovoi** numbers delves into the realm of advanced techniques and combinations.

Here, we weave a narrative that not only explains but also brings to life the complex sequences and their integration into daily life. Use it 28 times a day, or at least 3 times a day.

Chapter 6: Advanced Techniques and Combinations

In the intricate world of **Grabovoi** numbers, where each digit holds a universe of possibilities, advanced techniques are like the secret passages in a grand castle, leading to hidden chambers of profound change and manifestation. **71 931** is ht protection from negative information.

Complex Sequences for Specific and Advanced Goals

Imagine you are an artist, looking to not only create but to inspire and revolutionize. For such a lofty goal, simple number sequences might not suffice. Here, we employ a complex sequence like **485 14 85** – a symphony of digits, **against Migraine,** each resonating with creativity, inspiration, and influence. This sequence isn't just recited; it's woven into the very fabric of your creative process, a silent mantra that accompanies every stroke of the brush, every choice of color.

Integrating Numbers into Daily Routines and Practices

Integration of these powerful sequences into daily life can be as simple as it is profound. Consider a business person seeking to make ethical, impactful decisions. Each morning, as part of their routine, they might meditate on the sequence **591 718 31 998**, which resonates with ethical clarity and business acumen. This sequence becomes a part of their morning coffee ritual, a moment of reflection and intention-setting for the day.

Case Study: The Transformation of a Small Business

Let's take the example of a small bookstore struggling to survive in a digital age. The owner, armed with the sequence **318 514 517 618** for prosperity and **741 321 975** for overcoming challenges, begins to incorporate these numbers into every aspect of the business. From the way books are arranged (in groups reflecting these numbers) to the timing of promotional events (chosen based on numerological significance), the bookstore transforms. Slowly, it becomes a community hub, a place not just for buying books but for connection and growth – a success story woven from the very threads of **Grabovoi** numbers.

Expert Insights : improve your memory

Experts in **Grabovoi** numbers suggest that the power of these sequences lies not just in their recitation but in their embodiment. It's about living the numbers, letting them resonate in every action, decision, and thought. As one expert puts it, *"Grabovoi numbers are not just to be used; they are to be lived. They are the music to which your life dances."* **Try 589 32 40 to improve your memory.**

Numerical Sequences in Grabovoi codes : 0121 manifest new job

There are many testimonials and real-life examples of successful implementations of these codes that demonstrate their power and effectiveness. For example, one person used the Number Sequence **1144** to help them manifest a promotion at Number Sequence **0121** to manifest a new job and saw results within days. Another person used the Number Sequence **5678** to increase their creativity and soon started having new creative ideas. These are just two examples of the many successful implementations of **Grabovoi Codes.**

HORMONES / HORMONAS / гормоны

In Chapter 7, we venture forth with the same lively spirit, exploring the future horizon of **Grabovoi** numbers. This chapter, painted with the strokes of Twain's humor, Saunders' inventiveness, and Ephron's insightful wit, casts a visionary gaze upon the unfolding journey of these mystical numbers. You can achieve everything which you put in **intention with 894 719 78 48** and do not forget **ease your stress with 819 471. For exemple you can master your MIND & hormones :**

Adrenaline or Epinephrine (energy)   531 42 18 4161
Boosts fight-or-flight response, increasing heart rate and energy.
French. Adrénaline
Spanish: Adrenalina
Russian: Адреналин

Dopamine (mood, pleasure)   582 15 45
Neurotransmitter linked to pleasure, motivation, and reward.
French: Dopamine
Spanish: Dopamina
Russian: Допамин

Oxytocin (love, attachment)   319 48 12 961
Promotes bonding, trust, and social connections.
French: "Ocytocine"
Spanish: "Oxitocina"
Russian: "Окситоцин"

Serotonin (anxiety, depression, sleep)   514 81 23
Regulates mood, anxiety, and happiness.
French: Sérotonine
Spanish: Serotonina
Russian: Серотонин

Chapter 7: The Future of Grabovoi Numbers

As we stand at the threshold of tomorrow, the world of **Grabovoi** numbers shimmers with potential, like a star-studded sky awaiting exploration. This isn't just a tale of what will be; it's a canvas of possibilities, a symphony of future harmonies, for you and the humanity.

The Evolution of Practices and Applications

Imagine a future where **Grabovoi** numbers are as commonplace as smartphones, where their sequences are taught in schools alongside algebra and literature. In this world, the application of numbers evolves beyond personal healing and abundance. They become tools for societal change, instruments in shaping policies, and catalysts in scientific discoveries. The numbers, once perceived as mystical, are now recognized as a universal language, bridging gaps between cultures, disciplines, and philosophies.

Integration into Modern Holistic and Alternative Therapies

In the clinics of the future, **Grabovoi** numbers integrate seamlessly with holistic and alternative therapies. Picture a healing session where acupuncture is complemented by specific numerical sequences, enhancing the flow of energy. Or imagine psychological therapy, where counselors use **Grabovoi** numbers to deepen insights and foster healing.

These numbers become an intrinsic part of wellness practices, offering a dimension of healing that transcends the physical, reaching into the realms of the energetic and spiritual.

Expanding Community and Global Impact

As the community of **Grabovoi** practitioners expands, so does its impact on the world stage. We see a global network of individuals and groups, connected not just by a shared practice but by a collective vision for a better world. This community transcends borders, creating a tapestry of cooperation and understanding that weaves through continents and cultures.

In this interconnected world, **Grabovoi** numbers become a universal language of healing and transformation. They are used in peace negotiations, in environmental restoration projects, and in initiatives to bridge socioeconomic divides. The numbers resonate not just with individuals but with the heartbeat of the planet, echoing a message of hope and unity.

The Dance of Numbers and Humanity

As we peer into the crystal ball of the future, we see a dance – a dance of numbers and humanity, twirling together towards a horizon of limitless potential. In this dance, the numbers are more than just tools; they are partners, guiding us towards a future where harmony, understanding, and holistic wellness are not just ideals, but realities.

In this chapter, we've painted a vision of the future of **Grabovoi** numbers – a future where their application and influence extend far beyond personal use, becoming a cornerstone in the ongoing quest for a harmonious, healthy, and interconnected world. This narrative is not just a projection; it's an invitation to a future where the magic of numbers plays a central role in shaping our collective destiny.

The recognition and acceptance of **Grigori Grabovoi's** teachings, including his number system, can vary significantly depending on cultural, geographical, and individual contexts. It's important to note that while **Grabovoi**'s methods have found a following and have been discussed in various circles, they remain part of alternative belief systems.

The realm of alternative beliefs and practices often sees shifts in popularity and acceptance, and it's possible that **Grabovoi's** teachings have gained more attention or followers in Eastern countries.

The core principles for evaluating practices like the **Grabovoi** number system are still based on <u>scientific evidence and research</u>. However, these principles haven't been thoroughly applied to the **Grabovoi** method, perhaps due to its Russian origins.

Choose a code and say it out loud while imagining that what you want to happen is already real. Feel **gratitude** for what you have and what you want to receive.

Elimination of Negativity   **548 491 698 719**
Élimination de la Négativité
Eliminación de la Negatividad
Устранение Негатива

Vaccine Protection (*very useful since March 2020*)   **44 88 96 76 749**
Protection vaccinale (très utile depuis mars 2020)
Protección vacunal (muy útil desde marzo de 2020)
Вакцинальная защита (очень полезно с марта 2020 года)

As for how to use Grabovoi Numbers, the key is:

Repeat your **Grabovoi** sequence & repeat the numbers in your head, 28 times is a must, at least 20 minutes a day.

- Focus on the numbers by looking at them for 5 minutes.

- <u>Memories the sequence and repeat them back multiple times during the day, unit by unit.</u>

- **Write it** on a piece of paper... repeat <u>28 times.</u>

- **<u>Visualise the numbers</u>** <u>and you manifesting the desire</u>

- Imagine the number sequence coming from a ray of light or burst of energy.

- Picture the numbers in 3D and the color sliver.

- **Write the numbers on paper, then put a glass of water on top of the paper.** Water has incredible energy transfer powers. More than you think.

- **<u>Write the numbers (719) on a drinking bottle and drink the water.</u>** You are absorbing the number sequences and energy from the water simultaneously.

- Design a screen saver for your mobile phone with your number sequence. On average, we check our mobile phones 100 times daily.

- Create a subliminal track with your **Grabovoi** numbers playing at a subliminal frequency below consciousness.
- Picked a manifestation crystal related to your desire and write the number on it. Carry the crystal in your pocket and touch it multiple times a day.

*I wish you , all the best. Everything is Possible (**519 71 48**)*

Visualize these numbers, it works.

Have faith in the power of the codes.

Be safe.

520 741 8 + 888 412 128 90 18 3*

Christophe Paroni

* Abundance + Love

Other Spiritual Enlightenment Books by Christophe Paroni

<u>*From the same author, Christophe Paroni (in French)*</u>

PCR, Covid-19: *LA Supercherie Planétaire (ed. 2020)*
CO2, *Du Pass Sanitaire au Pass Co2, Le Grand Bullshit! (ed. 2021)*
NIGER: *L'Ombre de la Russie, la France est virée. (ed. 2023)*
LA VACHE NE RIT PLUS : *Les Insectes débarquent (ed.2023)*
Les 20 Prophéties pour l'Europe : *2024-2028 (ed.2023)*
L'ÂME contre la Matrice *(ed. 2024)*
L'EAU Quantique *(ed.2024)*
GRABOVOI : La Matrice qui guérit ! *(Ed.2024)*

<u>*From the same author , Christophe Paroni (in English)*</u>

UFO-UPA *The Fabric of our Reality.*
ICT : *Mastering Market Algos with ICT methodology*
ICE : *Everything is Illusion*
WAR : *The War over Power : Energy Conflict in the Age*
  of Putin Fueling the Fire : the Precipice of WWIII
AI : *The New Internet - Chat GPT*
9: *Hacking Number 9 : The Magic of 9*
I'M ENOUGH - <u>the law of retroaction</u>
2024 Mirage: TRUMP , *Rigged Election & The Inevitable War*
TESLA : *Revolution on Wheels : Unstoppable Tesla*
BLUE. *BLUE is EVERYTHING*

*This book is dedicated to **Gregori Grabovoï, Angela, Alexis, Luisito, Maguy, Bernard, Céline**, and all those I may have inadvertently forgotten. Take care of yourselves; everything is written in the Universe.*

*Ce livre est dédié à **Gregori Grabovoï, Angela, Alexis, Luisito, Maguy, Bernard, Céline**, et à tous ceux que j'ai pu oublier involontairement. Prenez soin de vous ; tout est écrit dans l'Univers.*

*Este libro está dedicado a **Gregori Grabovoï, Angela, Alexis, Luisito, Maguy, Bernard, Céline**, y a todos aquellos que pude haber olvidado sin querer. Cuídense; todo está escrito en el Universo.*

*Эта книга посвящается **Григорию Грабовому, Анжеле, Алексису, Луисито, Магуи, Бернарду**, Селин и всем тем, кого я мог случайно забыть. Берегите себя; все написано во Вселенной.*

Made in United States
Troutdale, OR
10/29/2024